ABOUT THE NEW WORLD AFRICAN PRESS

The New World African Press has evolved over a period of 15 years. Originally, it began as Elsie Mae Enterprises in honor of my own special guiding light, the late Elise Mae Hadnot Holloway. Later, Elsie Mae Enterprises was changed to the Boniface I Obichere Press in honor of my late mentor, friend and colleague, who passed from this realm making his transition to the afterlife in 1997.

The Boniface I. Obichere Press metamorphosed into the New World African Press in 2000. While the name of the Press has gone through several name changes, its mission and purpose has remained the same. As such, it fills the void and reverses the neglect of the major publishing houses as it provides a venue for books on the Diasporic experiences in Africa, Europe and the New World. While the New World African Press purpose is primarily Diasporic in nature, it is also committed to publishing non-Diasporic works and literature.

It is an honor and a privilege for the New World African Press to publish *Jellemoh*, an important biography written by the late Dr. Mary Antoinette Brown Sherman about the life and times of her mother.

I first met Dr. Sherman in 1989 when I was a Visiting Scholar at Cornell University at the Africana Center. She met with me almost daily to discuss Liberian issues and the biography she was writing about her mother, Victoria Elizabeth Jellemoh Grimes. Our path crossed from a distance in 1980 when she was the President of the University of Liberia and I was scheduled to come to Liberia on a Fullbright Fellowship. She remembered my application passing her desk. Unfortunately, a bloody coup against the Tolbert regime occurred and my Fellowship was cancelled by the State Department.

I am truly thankful for Dr. Mary Antoinette Brown Sherman friendship, scholarship and spiritual support while I was at Cornell, the most memorable time in my life. I learned much from her and her late husband the Honorable G. Flamma Sherman.

Joseph E. Holloway, Ph.D.
CEO Editor-in-Chief of the
New World African Press

First New Edition, 2005

Publisher:
New World African Press
1958 Matador Way Unit #35
Northridge, CA 91330

ISBN 0-9768761-0-8

Published by the New World African Press
ALL RIGHTS RESERVED

The New World African Press books are printed in the United States of America on acid-free paper and meet the guidelines for permanence and durability of the committee on production guidelines for book longevity of the council on Library resources.

Printed in the United States of America. All rights reserved. No part of this publication may be reproduced or transmitted in any form or by any means, electronic or mechanical, including photocopying, recording, or by an information storage and retrieval system - except by a reviewer.

Although the author and publisher have made every effort to ensure the accuracy and completeness of the materials. The Press assumes no responsibility for errors, inaccuracies, omissions, or any inconsistency herein.

JELLEMOH

A Story of the Life and Times of Victoria Elizabeth Jellemoh Grimes,
A Liberian Wife and Mother

By

Mary Antoinette Brown Sherman

TABLE OF CONTENTS

Table of Contents		
Preface		i
Introduction		v
Chapter 1	Birth and Early Experiences	1
Chapter 2	Acquiring an Education for Living	7
Chapter 3	Chosen to Become a Bride	12
Chapter 4	Wedding Bells and a Musu Tombo	15
Chapter 5	Carving a Niche in Monrovia	17
Chapter 6	Wife and Mother in a Liberian Extended Family	23
Chapter 7	Example and Precepts - Vic's Guiding Words	43
Chapter 8	A Treasure Taken Away	51
Chapter 9	Adjusting to Life Without Louis	54
Chapter 10	Final Days - "The End of Us All"	67
Chapter 11	A Summing Up	73
Notes		75
Bibliography		79
Appendices		81

Appendix	I	Marriage Certificate of Louis A. Grimes and Ms. Victoria E. Cheeseman
Appendix	II	Members of the Culture Club, Monrovia
Appendix	III	A Tribute to my Mother Victoria Elizabeth Grimes by Henry W. Grimes
Appendix	IV	Vic's Guiding Words
Appendix	V	Children of Louis Arthur Grimes and Victoria Elizabeth Jellemoh Grimes

PREFACE

One morning in 1994, as Mother's Day approached, I had the interesting experience of awakening with words flashing across my mind. These words would impel me to begin to write this story of my mother's life and times and would appear as the opening sentence of the story.

The idea of writing about her was not new. It was stimulated to some extent as far back as April, 1970, when *The Liberian Official Gazette*, vol. xlix, no. 4, was released at the time of her death. Through this document, interest in her as a biographical subject would develop, especially among scholars - an interest that would remain alive for the next decades.

My own thinking about her in this light emerged as I increasingly reflected on the Liberian society following the 1980 coup d'etat in Liberia. Hailing as she did from indigenous roots in our society, I could not help feeling that a focus on her would be valuable in itself. It would also contribute to understanding the social history of our country, on which little had been written, and to appreciating the Liberian reality. Her positive approach to life stood out in my mind in sharp contrast to the negative images we were getting from people of indigenous background who had been catapulted to leadership positions in our country by the coup. What made for a positive self - concept and positive contributions to society, I wondered - religious beliefs, family background, home training, education, societal linkages, a combination of two or more of these? But the times were troublous, and I found myself too consumed with the challenges of leadership at the University of Liberia to turn reflections into biographical writing.

The decade of violence and unrest that ensued resulted in the destruction of much valuable archival material, family papers and family memorabilia and my desire for such writing faded. Meanwhile, there was a transformation in my life situation as I became primary caregiver for my husband, G. Flamma Sherman, diagnosed with Alzheimer's disease in August, 1990. Despite these major handicaps, the continuing interest of a long-time friend of mine and fellow educator, Adelaide M. Cromwell, Director Emerita of the African American Studies Center of Boston University, made her broach the subject. The history of Liberia she felt needed to be personalized and I did have my memory. I realized too that there were family members, friends and others whose memories I could tap. However, it took that divine inspiration to spur me to action.

i

I have used my own memory and, through telephone conversations, interviews and letters, have drawn from the memories of a number of persons who knew my mother and were close to her in various ways - consanguinal and affinal relatives, friends and other knowledgeable people. They shared with me generously of their memories of her, my father, relatives of the two of them, her relationships and her life and work in Edina and Monrovia. I deeply appreciate their doing so.

Key among consanguinal relatives were: my brother, J. Rudolph Grimes; my first cousin, Albert Kini Freeman and his daughter, Mary Victoria Hawa Freeman; my first cousin, Irene Wiles; and the important Kiazolu link, Augustus Feweh Caine. Rudolph who sharpened my thinking, sharing precise information, especially about the years just preceding and the early years of the marriage of our parents. Kini and Hawa broadened my knowledge of my maternal history and shared other important information. From Irene came details of interest in my paternal history. Feweh etched large the relationship of his father to my mother and the benefits to her as well as him and his children. Underlying his account was the Kiazolu tie.

Of affinal relatives, the key ones whose memories I tapped were my sister-in-law, Rosina Grimes; my foster sisters, Edna Zoe Freeman, Christine Richards and Gladys Smith; Wannie Cooper, niece of my foster sister, Elsie Frank Simmonds; and Liamon Doe, daughter of my foster brother, Jackson Doe. Each contributed valuable information, especially Zoe, who from Sweden where she was then based, spent many precious hours corresponding with me, answering questions and volunteering information and also trying to convey her deep feeling for her foster parents. The interest she manifested in having this story written helped to propel me as I wrote.

Two other affinal relatives who were especially helpful were Mrs. Martha Cooper and her daughter, Williette Summerville Cooper, direct descendants of S. G. Harmon, husband of the younger sister of my mother's foster mother. They provided interesting information on my mother's foster parents. In addition, Mrs. Cooper, a contemporary of my mother, although years younger, gave a feel for the Edina of their day.

Another important contributor to this story was Corinna Hilton van Ee, who was born in Monrovia about 10 years after my mother married and settled in Monrovia. Daughter of a close friend of my mother, she was able to provide information about her and the Monrovia of her day from the perspective of one of a younger generation. Adeline Neal was especially helpful in providing information regarding my mother's connection with the Eastern Star. Others whose memories I tapped were Maude Freeman Todd, whose first husband was my first cousin, George Molondoi Freeman, who predeceased her; Emmett Harmon, a foster brother; Antoinette Tubman, Mai Roberts and Florence Peal, cousins; Horace Gibson and Isabel Karnga, children of two of my father's classmates (Liberia College, Class of 1903); Jessye Togba, one of the close associates of my mother in the work of the Antoinette Tubman Children's Welfare Foundation; and

Izetta Roberts Cooper, niece of Miss Alice Roberts, music teacher of three of the Grimes' children.

Relevant source materials on Liberia were not easy to come by. Thus, I am especially grateful to D. Elwood Dunn who led me to the archives of the Episcopal Church in the United States of America and information on the school my mother attended. I am also grateful to Debra Newman Ham who offered suggestions for locating Liberian newspapers published in the first decades of the 20th century. Due to gaps, this important source did not yield the results hoped for, but did point to another source.

I was greatly facilitated in my research by Stephanie Walker, Assistant Archivist for Reference Services, the Archives of the Episcopal Church, Austin, Texas. She provided me the records enabling me to link Brierly Memorial, the Episcopal school my mother attended, with its forerunners, the Orphan Asylum and the Boarding School for Native Girls and to fit this school into the history of Episcopal schools In Liberia. My thanks go to her and to the Archives of the Episcopal Church for permission to use quotations and pictures from their records.

Also facilitating my research was Virginia Parks, then Head of Reference Services at the Hillsborough Public Library, who, through inter-library loan, obtained for me valuable materials, among these, the Collection of the Honorable Louis A. Grimes, 1883-1948. My deepest thanks go to her and also to B. K. Robertson who assisted me by searching through issues of the Liberia Bulletin and other materials found in the Cornell University Library. Among materials he located there was the issue of the Liberian Law Reports which carries the historic case of Karmo versus Morris. My gratitude goes also to Reference Librarians of the Middletown Township Public Library for their work in locating materials for this research.

My sons, Kedrick W. Brown, Jr. (K. B.) and B. A. Marbue Brown, were enthusiastic about this venture and constantly encouraged me. After reading the first few pages of my draft, Marbue provided the technical support to keep me moving on and K. B. suggested after reading the first few pages that I expand the account into a book. My thanks go beyond words to them and to their respective wives, Constance (Connie) and Lena and their total of eight children (four for each couple) who provided the two home environments which enabled me to combine writing this story with the demands of caregiving for my husband. Added thanks go to K. B. and Connie for their contribution of several family pictures from their photo albums, filling in what otherwise would have been a big gap, as much of my collection was lost during the 1989-1997 Civil War in Liberia. To their daughter, Taanya Mokandai Brown, goes my gratitude for use of the drawing she made at age seven of her great grandmother.

My cousin, Rhoda Peal Zangai, did a casual reading of a portion of my initial draft and offered critical comments I found useful. Also reading a portion of the draft was Isabel Karnga. She offered helpful editorial suggestions. Adelaide M. Cromwell provided valuable editorial comments and suggestions on the entire draft. I appreciate the contribution of each of these three persons. My brother, J. Rudolph Grimes, read the entire draft and offered comments and suggestions which were insightful. I very much appreciate this additional contribution of his. C. E. Zamba Liberty, a professional colleague of mine from the 1970s when we both worked in administration and instruction at the University of Liberia, also read the entire draft. He provided valuable information, raised probing questions and offered insightful suggestions which helped me to shape the story and present my mother in the times and social context in which she lived. For his significant contribution, I am indebted beyond words and deeply grateful to him.

I alone, however, bear responsibility for the story as told and for any shortcomings it might have.

Mary Antoinette Brown Sherman
Nov. 30, 1997

INTRODUCTION

Literature written by Africans South of the Sahara in one of the European languages has only been taken seriously by the West in the last 50 years and of that literature, it is fair to say, that biography and autobiography have been the last to emerge and the least appreciated.

No attempt is being made here to survey the vast amount of literature by Africans, for since the 1960s the volume of this literature goes way beyond the possibility of coverage in an introductory essay. However, it is important to have some appreciation of the earlier roots and the trend in amount and orientation of African literature from the earliest documented period.

Portraits of Africans were the first form of published literature. These portraits were drawn in various ways. Published letters are a valuable source. *The Letter of the Late Ignatius Sancho* and the *Narrative of the Life of Oladuah Equiano or Gustavus Vassa,* The African were written in English and published in England in the last decades of the 18th century. In *Africa Remembered, Narratives by West Africans From the Era of the Slave Trade*, Philip Curtin, editor, Madison, University of Wisconsin, 1967, seven Africans described for posterity their personal experiences as former slaves. Included among the seven were the above mentioned Gustavus Vassa whose Memoirs were published in 1789, *Letters from Phillip Quaqué of Cape Coast*, the first African ordained as a priest of the Church of England and the well known Samuel Ajaya Crowther whose Letters to the Church Missionary Society were published in 1837. For most of the seven included in this volume the line between autobiographical and biographical writing is blurred. However, *The Life of Joseph Wright, A Native Ackoo* published in June 1839 is clearly an autobiography.

Anna Melissa Graves published letters from several Africans, including three women, whom she met on a trip to West Africa in 1930, (Anna Melissa Graves, ed., *Benvenuto Celini Had No Prejudice Against Bronze, Letters From West Africans*, Baltimore: Waverly Press, 1943).

Aside from these endeavors, the picture of Africans as persons is drawn largely in novels, plays, short stories and poetry. Casely Hayford's novel, *Ethiopia Unbound*, published in 1911 and *Batouala* by René Maran, published in 1921, are among the first autobiographical/biographical novels. Maran also wrote four other biographies, three of Europeans and one of Felix Eboué, the distinguished African Governor of Equatorial Africa (1951).

In the decades between 1920 and 1939, novels and biographies began to appear. *Guanya Pau, The Story of an African Princess* by Joseph Walter, a Liberian, published in 1891 was reputedly the first novel written in English. Varfelli Karlee (nom de plume of Charles Cooper), *Love in Ebony, A West African Romance*, published in 1932 as the second novel was also by a Liberian. Liberia's contribution to all literary genres over the years has been minimal, but Bai T. Moore, another Liberian, published the third autobiography, *Gola Boy in America* in 1937. The second autobiography, *Prince Nyabongo's The Story of an African Chief*, published in both English and Swahili in 1935, followed by one hundred and forty-six years the first already mentioned, the interesting *Narrative of the Life of Oladuah Equiano or Gustavus Vassa, The African.*

Aside from Bai T. Moore, only three other authors from Liberia are noted by Donald E. Herdeck in the book he edited on African authors (Donald E. Herdeck, editor, African Authors: *A Companion to Black African Writers*, Vol. 1, 1300 to 1973, Washington, D.C., Black Orpheus Press, 1973). They were: Roland Dempster, Wilton Sankawulo and Doris Henries, all three of whom published after the 1930s. Dempster's poems, "Echoes from a Valley," were published in 1947; Wilton Sankawulo's "The Evil Forest," a story, in 1971 and the writings of A. Doris Banks Henries in the 1960s. In 1962, she published *Heroes and Heroines of Liberia*, in 1966, Essays in Various Works and Journals, in 1967, *A Biography of President William V. S. Tubman* and in 1969, *Africa, Our History.*

Returning now to these earlier years, novels have appeared in French and Portuguese and a biographical novel in English, *Man of Africa*, by Samuel Ntara from Malawi appeared in 1934. While there is a definite increase in literary publications during the decades from 1940 to 1959, there were some seventeen novels published in French but only six published in English. However, during this same period there were seven autobiographies published in English and only one in French.

In the last decade chronicled by Herdeck, there was an unexpected shift in the language employed by the authors. During this period, there were forty-six novels published in English which far outnumbered those eight published in French or two in Portuguese. There were eight autobiographies published - all in English and all by men. There was, however, a growing body of literature in African languages and the only two biographies written were in African languages-one by a South African in Zulu in 1938 and the other by a Nigerian in 1951 in Hausa.

Since the 1970s several biographies have been written on political leaders but they are still few in number and do not include women. *Daughter of Africa* by Ruth Isabel Seabury published in 1945 about a South African woman and *Nzinga the Queen from Angola* by Roy Glascow in 1982 and in Portuguese are the two biographies of women until Adelaide M. Cromwell published *An African Victorian Feminist, The Life and Times of Adelaide Smith Casely Hayford* in 1986. Mrs. Casely Hayford had published a serialized autobiography in West African Review in 1953 and 1954.

However, the weekly journal West Africa beginning in 1953 until December, 1973, featured the lives of 19 women, only one Liberian, Ellen Mills Scarborough, who was featured in the Feb. 18, 1961, issue. Kenneth Dike published a collection of essays on eminent Nigerians of the nineteenth century, (Cambridge University Press, 1966). Among them was one woman, Madame Tinubu.

The mixture of biography and autobiography seems to characterize the literature on African women particularly. Mrs. Casely Hayford's portrait is one example. She had written her own story on which Cromwell relied rather heavily to write her biography. A second example of a mixed form is *Baba of Karo, A Woman of the Muslim Hausa*, by M. F. Smith (New York: Philosophical Library, 1955). Baba dictated the story of her life in Hausa to M. F. Smith who then translated it into English. Baba was from Zaria Province in Northern Nigeria. The dictation took a period of six weeks and the material was recorded verbatim as far as possible. Baba was an elderly Hausa woman willing to undertake the project of speaking of her life to an outsider when women were expected to be almost cloistered. Baba's story would never have been published without the intercession of M. F. Smith.

The other example of a mixture of autobiography and biography is the recently published Constance Agatha Cummins-John: *Memoirs of a Krio Leader*, edited with an introduction and annotation by La Ray Denzer (Sam Bookman, 1955). Mrs. Cummins-John, an educator and activist from Sierra Leone, tells her story her way but a broader interpretation is added.

It is against this scarcity of biographical writing on the one hand and the small number of Liberian writers on the other that *Jellemoh: The Story of the Life and Times of Victoria Elizabeth Jellemoh, A Liberian Wife and Mother* by her daughter, Mary Antoinette Brown Sherman, is most welcome and important. Furthermore, it is in a sense ironic that it is from Liberia in its period of tragic history when even the state itself seems on the verge of collapse that a biography reflecting optimism and hope should appear.

Mary Antoinette Grimes Brown Sherman, a scholar and educator and former president of the University of Liberia, has written a warm and valuable biography of her mother, Victoria Elizabeth Jellemoh Grimes. Mrs. Grimes was born in February, 1889, a member of the Kiazolu clan of her father in the village of Jondu, Gawula Chiefdom, Cape Mount, Liberia and died on April 19, 1970, in Monrovia, as a highly revered person and widow of the distinguished Secretary of State Louis Arthur Grimes, Chief Justice at the time of his death in 1948.

Recently, Liberian history has worked in a paradoxical way to make possible this excellent biography, for without the chaos and destruction in Liberia, Dr. Sherman might not have had the time to devote to this project. Yet because Liberia has suffered war and destruction during the last seven years, the records and other documents and pictures usually available to and needed for research were either destroyed or inaccessible to Dr. Sherman. Like so many of her country persons she left her country and settled in the United States, with her husband,

vii

sons and their families. However, in spite of this adversity, building on the resources available in the United States, she was able to utilize to the fullest the memories of an extraordinarily wide circle of relatives and friends in Liberia, the United States and Europe. By so doing, she gave her mother's life an historical intimacy and the reader a more expansive knowledge of the dimensions of Liberian life and culture during that period.

Beginning with her birth in a village to indigenous parents, her early adoption by Liberia's President Joseph James Cheeseman and his wife, Mary Ann, the little girl was early exposed to the sophisticated life of Monrovia under the most prestigious auspices. When President Cheeseman suddenly died, his widow returned to their home town, Edina. Victoria was temporarily reconnected with her parents and thus she began reestablishing ties with her traditional heritage - ties that remained with her throughout her life, including fluency in Vai, her mother tongue.

Victoria Elizabeth Jellemoh was, however, returned to Mrs. Cheeseman and remained with her, attending Brierly Memorial, an Episcopal boarding school for girls in Harper, Cape Palmas and also acquired some business and hand-working skills as well as a love for music. She was always comfortable in the two worlds; the traditional or village Liberia, kept so by her uncle, Chief Varney Marbue of Jondu and Chief Boima Njoh of Vai Town and in the world of Americo-Liberians, more accurately described as the élite society of Monrovia. Her marriage to Louis A. Grimes, a member of the distinguished Barclay family whose parents immigrated to Liberia from Barbados, gave her a secure position in Monrovia.

It is the obligation of Africans themselves based on their own experiences or those of other Africans to tell the rest of the world, which often means Africans from other countries, what it was really like to grow up and live in a particular African setting. Myths and falsehoods have distorted our understanding of African life as it is experienced on a day-to-day basis, both in the past as well as today. This close view of Victoria Elizabeth Jellemoh's life reveals that there was a bond between tribal up-country Liberians and the more Westernized people of the coast, that while Christianity and Western education were highly valued they were not necessarily in conflict with traditional values. The renowned reputation of the importance of the extended family composed of blood related, adopted and foster children was truly the strength of the people.

Victoria Elizabeth Jellemoh's life is enlightening for validating all of these points but all the more so because as a woman, never stepping out beyond that role, one learns from it how a wife, mother and citizen live and experience the joys, hopes, frustrations and tragedies which reveal the similarity more than the differences between her life and ours. Her anxiety over her husband's travels abroad, her pain at the death of her oldest son at the age of seven and the death of her talented youngest son at the age of fourteen in a swimming accident, her excitement as a bride to move from her in-laws' home to her own home and her reluctance as a widow to leave her home for her daughter's when age and infirmity made it a rational decision. Of course, there were strains to overcome from being "Mrs. Cheeseman's Vai Girl" to achieving a position in the élite society of Monrovia and maintaining a close bond with her sister Pai, who had been reared by their natural parents in the traditional way and spoke no English.

Louis Arthur Grimes was an important influence in Victoria Elizabeth Jellemoh's life. As an eligible young lawyer in Monrovia who had been exposed to the philosophy of Edward Wilmot Blyden, eminent scholar and teacher, who believed that the fabric of life in Monrovia would be strengthened if there were intermarriage between Americo-Liberians and the tribal Liberians, Grimes, according to his daughter, was attracted to Victoria Elizabeth Jellemoh for her personal qualities which included being rooted in the traditional culture and preferred her over the exclusively Western-oriented young women in Monrovia. Even their marriage ceremony was performed twice - once according to the Western way in the St. Luke Episcopal Church in Edina and two months later also in Jondu according to the rites of the Vai people.

Louis Arthur Grimes was just the right person to find happiness with Victoria Elizabeth Jellemoh. He learned Vai to be comfortable with her people and yet he was sophisticated enough as a lawyer to plead Liberia's cause at the League of Nations in the early 1930s. Louis and Victoria Elizabeth Jellemoh were the parents of five children of their own. They also reared the only grandchild they had at the time of Louis' death on Dec. 14, 1948, and 20 foster children from six ethnic groups. Their other grandchildren - eight - arrived after his death.

Living in Monrovia as the wife of a distinguished lawyer, Victoria Elizabeth Jellemoh was an active participant in the society of that city. She was a member of the Culture Club of Monrovia organized about 1918 and composed of young women who set standards in etiquette and involved themselves in community projects. She was also a key figure in the Eastern Star, sister organization of the Ancient, Free and Accepted Masons and such voluntary agencies as the Girl Guides, the YWCA and the Antoinette Tubman Children's Welfare Foundation. A deeply religious person, she was a member of Trinity Church in Monrovia from the time of her marriage to her death.

Compared with the opportunities afforded African women today, Victoria was not a widely traveled person, but she did visit Sierra Leone in the 1920s as part of an official visiting party from Liberia and when Mary Antoinette joined her husband Kedrick Brown who was sent in 1950 as Financial Attaché to the Liberian Embassy in Washington, she traveled with her daughter in 1951 to visit them. Going by boat, the trip was memorable for both because of their stops in Holland, Switzerland, France and England.

Mary Antoinette was the only daughter of Louis Arthur and Victoria Elizabeth Jellemoh and knew her mother well, for aside from the above mentioned sojourn in the United States and two study periods in the United States she was always nearby. She provides the reader through this biography with a closer feeling for her mother through the "Excerpts and Precepts" her mother spoke frequently to her children -- "An idle hand is the devil's workshop," "When you do your best, no more is required; or other less familiar to ones in the West - "Liquor in, wits out." But the ones which obviously made the greatest impression on her daughter were "Mr. Talk is all right but Mr. Do is the Man" and "Don't take the last pea out of the pod."

This story of Victoria Elizabeth Jellemoh Grimes' life is a welcome addition to the small amount of biographical writing on Africans - and on women in particular, but appearing as it does when Liberia is in such turmoil gives one reason to hope that the future for this country can still be bright if from its population emerge women with the character and intelligence of Victoria Elizabeth Jellemoh Grimes.

Adelaide M. Cromwell
Director Emeritus
African-American Studies Center
Boston University

CHAPTER 1

Birth and Early Experiences

Images a bridge evokes - linkage, strength, accessibility - brings vividly to my mind my mother, Victoria Elizabeth Jellemoh. Born in February, 1889, in the traditional world of the village of Jondu, Gawula Chiefdom, Cape Mount, Liberia, she entered Liberian "sophisticated society"[1] as a little child through Liberia's President Joseph James Cheeseman and his wife, Mary Ann. Increased relationships were thereby facilitated between people of the Vai indigenous ethnic group and the "new world" settlers who landed in the 1820s on the shores of West Africa's Grain Coast, which later came to be known as Liberia.

Jellemoh was the first of two children of her parents, Ambollai and Jarsie Fahnbulleh, to survive infancy and spare them the pain of infant deaths which they had experienced after several successive births from their union. The name she was given, Jellemoh, communicated their sense of despair. It signified that she was not to stay with them. However, by a miracle of God, she beat the odds and transformed their sad expectations into hope and joy. About two years after her birth, a second child, Hawa Pai, arrived and, by her survival, provided another surprise, adding to the joy of their parents. Jellemoh and Hawa Pai outlived their parents, each of their lives spanning more than the three score years and ten promised in the Bible. They were separated for most of their childhood but reunited as young adults, maintaining after their reunion a close relationship until Jellemoh's death nearly six decades later. Through their surviving children and the succeeding generations of grandchildren and great grandchildren, they live on, close ties intact.

When Jellemoh was born in Jondu (Vai word meaning slave town), the town was still one of the important towns in the Vai country. Jondu had become an important center, partly because, during the slave trading period, it was a place where enslaved Africans were held for exchange and sale. Its importance was also due to the fact that it was there that Dwalu Bukere and his five relatives - his brother, Dshara Barakora and their cousins Dshara Kali, Kali Bara, Fa Gbasi and So Tabaku invented the Vai system of syllabic writing in the 1840s. There in Jondu, their place of residence, they established the first school for teaching the system of writing and ran it for 17 months - until an outbreak of war forced them to seek refuge in Tombe.[2] By then, there were a number of graduates who would preserve and pass down the script mainly through letters, but also diaries, traditional tales, travelogues and autobiographies. A notable example is the autobiog-

1

raphy written by Ndolo Wono, one of the first graduates, acknowledged by scholars as a remarkable piece of literature. It is said to have included in addition to Wono's life story words of wisdom to the young.

According to legend, during the reign of Manja Gotola, in the Gawula country, Cape Mount, Bukele saw the characters of the Vai script in a dream. He was given a book and shown how to write words in the same characters in which the book was written. He reported that when he awoke, he could not remember all the characters he had seen and, therefore, he requested the assistance of several relatives. They helped him fill in the blanks and together they produced the Vai script. This system of syllabic writing is an original contribution to written languages. It made the Vais special in Liberia and gave them a unique place in history, as it is one of the earliest African ethnic groups to have its own system of writing. Into this rich heritage, Jellemoh was born and learned to take pride.

The Vai script was an important means of communication among the Vais. It also became known beyond the borders of Liberia early after its invention. German missionaries of the Church Missionary Society of the Church of England heard about the script shortly after its invention, while engaged around that time in West African language study at Fourah Bay College in nearby Sierra Leone. One of their members, Rev. Sigismund W. Koelle, traveled to Liberia, visited the area and observed the script in use by the people. He was impressed by this invention, became interested in it and began studying it. In 1849, he produced a grammar of the Vai language, five years before his *Polyglotta Africana*. From the time of Koelle's visit, the Germans exhibited interest in the Vai language and its script. By the 1920s, Vai had been introduced and was taught at Hamburg University, the first Liberian to be appointed Consul General to Germany (1922-1929), Momolu Massaquoi, a Vai, being one of those who taught the language there. He would influence Professor August Klingenheben of that University who, from then on, became involved in studying, learning, writing and teaching the Vai language and script. The Germans, it is believed, made use of the language during World War II, introducing a code in Vai that was never broken.

Jellemoh's life began in Jondu as a member of the Kiazolu clan of her father, a ruling clan of the Vais and one of the 11 original families which settled in what became Vai territory.[3] However, her life in this setting was short, for her early years practically coincided with the sofa kelleh (sofa war) and the destruction of Gawula by the famous warrior Chieftain Sofa Julla. A widespread inter-ethnic conflict which touched both Liberia and Sierra Leone, the sofa kelleh occurred between 1891 and 1895 and was one of the challenges the Cheeseman administration faced. It began when warriors connected with Samouri Toure, ruler of an empire in the Savannah region which corresponds roughly with present-day Guinea and Mali, responded to the call of the Manding ruler, Semolu, for help in a dispute against his neighbors, the Gola ethnic group of Liberia.[4] As the Golas and Vais had close connections, lived in adjoining territory, occasionally sharing the same territory, the Vais also suffered from the effects of the war. The sofa warriors reportedly acted independently once they entered the area, swept it and threw it into chaos. The Liberian Government was slow to respond and did so only after repeated calls from citizens of Robertsport, in the coastal area of Cape Mount, who felt their settlement was in danger and wanted the Government to intervene in the conflict so that peace and order could be restored. By late 1895, through a combination of force and negotiation, the Government was able to end this inter-ethnic conflict.[5]

During the conflict, infants and other small children were separated from their parents and held as prisoners. Among them were Jellemoh and her sister, Pai. As peace began to be restored to the area, they and others were recovered at Bong-ma and sent to the Superintendent of Cape Mount. When President Cheeseman, who had recently lost his last surviving child, Victoria Elizabeth, visited Cape Mount, he was so much reminded of this child by Jellemoh that he selected her to be fostered by himself and his wife who was still grieving over their loss. They named her Victoria Elizabeth after the child they had lost and her new home became that of the Cheeseman's in Liberia's Executive Mansion in Monrovia, the capital of Liberia. It was years later when things had settled in the area that her parents learned of her whereabouts, went to search for her and were able to find her in Edina, Grand Bassa County.

A different environment and many new experiences became Victoria's lot in her new home, among them, a shift in language from her mother tongue, the Liberian language, Vai, to English and in religion to the Christian religion which became an undergirding force in her life. While knowledge of English had distinct advantages, being cut off from her mother tongue at an early age had its problems. For example, Vai was not the language in which she communicated with her children when we arrived years later, an anomaly. Thus, for us, her "mother tongue" was not our first language.

Her Christian exposure began in the home. The family prayers her foster parents held, which included not only the children of the home but also the servants, had their impact. Then, there was the influence of the Baptist Church, her foster parents being Baptists. In fact, at the time she became a part of the Cheeseman family, President Cheeseman was also President of the Liberia Baptist Missionary Convention (now Liberia Baptist Missionary and Educational Convention), his tenure in that Office, 1881-1896, partly coinciding with his period as President of the nation (1892-1896). Having begun his period of service as Pastor of the First Baptist Church in Edina in 1868, when he was 25 years old and about three years after his marriage, he and his wife had given years of service to the Baptist work in Liberia.

Victoria had hardly comfortably settled in her new home when death struck and the home was filled with sadness. Her foster father, President Cheeseman, died in Office on Nov. 12, 1896. He was buried in his hometown, Edina. His widow vacated the Executive Mansion and a few months later, in 1897, returned to Edina, with Victoria and five other children she and her husband had been fostering.

Edina, one of the earliest settlements under the Colonization movement in the Grain Coast area, was settled in 1832 - 10 years after the first group of emigrants from the "new world" landed on Providence Island and eight years after the area acquired the name, Liberia. It was then the principal city and capital of Grand Bassa County and remained so for a number of decades after settlement. It was also important in trade and transportation throughout the 19th century and during the early 20th century because of its situation at the mouth of the St. John River, one of five main water-courses in the country at that time.[6] This was a period when rivers were the main transportation links and trail-and-river routes were the main thoroughfares.

In Edina, Victoria, then eight years old, began another period of adjustment. It could not have been easy, but she had the tender care of a loving foster mother, whom she always remembered with warmth and spoke about with love and affection. Under her, she spent most of the next 14 years growing up. This period was punctuated with studies at an Episcopal boarding school for girls situated in Harper, Cape Palmas. Educational opportunities in Liberia being extremely limited at the time, especially for girls, no doubt the quality of the school weighed heavier in her foster mother's decision regarding formal schooling for her than such problems as the distance she had to travel and the separation she had to endure from those to whom she had grown close.

The other break in her Edina stay occurred when her parents discovered where she was, went for her and took her back to the Vai country to be with them. However, Augustus Fahnwullu Caine, a Kiazolu, had spent a number of years working in the Bassa area for the trading firm, Oost Afrikaansche Compagnie (OAC) and accumulating some means for himself. He knew her foster mother and how this child was blossoming under her care. Through his persuasion and also with the assistance of the Government's Interior Department, she was voluntarily returned to her foster mother. Fahnwullu felt that left with her foster mother she would one day be of service to the Kiazolu people. To withdraw her was to let her lose a golden opportunity. Little did he dream, however, that he would benefit directly. That was the case when decades later, after he returned to Cape Mount to live, he was falsely implicated in the atrocities the Human Leopard Society had committed and was arrested. Through the influence of Jellemoh and her husband, he got proper representation in the investigations that took place and his release. He was able to go back to Bassa and spend his last days.

Fahnwullu also tried to get Pai, discovered about the same time, returned to the family fostering her, but Ambollai and Jarsie decided to keep her, the younger child and let Jellemoh, the older, go. Thus, development of the sisters along separate lines preceded - Victoria in the Western-oriented Liberian "sophisticated society" and Pai in traditional Vai society. Naturally, there was the common pain of separation, but the different settings posed problems and challenges for them that were contrary in nature. As adults, they sometimes reminisced about this situation.

One thing that stood out was Pai's regret that she had been denied the opportunity to remain a part of Liberian "sophisticated society." She never went to the Western-oriented school, nor did she learn to speak English. This was a constant reminder to Victoria that she could have been the one so denied and it must have given her the resolve to share the benefits derived from her foster parents and the home of herself and her husband with Pai and her children. Well-equipped, her foster parents and her life experiences had prepared her for the role of big sister.

Victoria's foster mother, Mary Ann, was a Crusoe. Her older brothers were the well-known Crusoe brothers who, by the time of Mary Ann's marriage in 1865, had carved for themselves a place as traders in Grand Bassa County and the nation. In fact, they and their father were among the 19th century merchants who through their economic power had the influence that contributed to balance in the political life of Liberia. Her husband, too, had been a successful merchant before becoming immersed in the political life of the nation, rising from small beginnings in trade. It was natural that Mary Ann, removed from the center of national life with the death of her husband, would find an outlet in something of which she had some knowledge and experience - trading. The business she established involved buying for export such domestic products which were important in foreign trade at the time, as piassava, camwood, palm kernels and coffee and importing fineries for ladies, such as hats and items of clothing which she sold in a store she owned and operated. The economic success she experienced helped her to become a powerful albeit silent force in the politics of Grand Bassa County and in national politics. Although women did not enjoy suffrage in Liberia at the time, her support of a politician from the area, who was interested in serving on the national scene, invariably led to his winning the election for a seat in the national Legislature.

The Cheeseman home, Mechlin House, was desirably located for trading - at the mouth of the St. John River, accessible by boats and by overland trail. It was a two-story structure of brickwork, with an attic. It was built on large logs, high enough to form a cellar. The building, the first floor of which was used as a store and the other floor as living quarters, had a commanding view of the river and the ocean. Victoria watched on a number of occasions when the oarsmen rowed out in surfboats to ships to carry products which were being exported. They traveled in groups of boats, always led by a "Headman," that is, the person who steered the first boat and after whom the boat was named. There being neither a natural nor a man-made harbor in the area at that time, ships anchored where they could safely play - in the deep of the ocean - and the boats rowed out to meet them. The boats had to travel through a sandbar which could be treacherous, especially in stormy weather when the swells from the ocean were rough and heavy. Victoria listened as discussions were held before the boats traveled out to the ships. The "Headman" made the decision based on the knowledge he acquired over years of practical experience. He noted the weather condition, watched the movement of the waves, counted the swells and studied their patterns and decided whether or not it was safe to venture out with the boats entrusted to his care. His success was measured by the number of trips he made to the ships and returned without a boat capsizing and his fame grew with each trip he made without losing a boat. Through listening and observation, Victoria began to appreciate the importance of indigenous skills, confirming, as it were, Malinowski's observation, that every society has its magic and religion and its science.[7] Indeed, the "Headmen" exhibited a scientific attitude to their environment and demonstrated a scientific knowledge of their setting. Victoria marveled.

CHAPTER 2

More Early Education Experiences

The experience acquired by observing and listening to the oarsmen and those who engaged their services constituted an aspect of informal education for Victoria. Not only did she glean information but also she began to sharpen two skills that would serve her well in the future - observing and listening. This experience and several other experiences converged in this setting to provide her a good informal education. For example, the language of daily intercourse in this part of the country was mainly the Liberian language, Bassa. This she acquired as she dealt with the oarsmen, the traders and the ordinary people with whom she came in contact. Thus, she learned a third language and her opportunities for interaction and learning expanded. While English was the official language of Liberia and the medium of instruction in the formal schools, there were many at that time who could not speak it and could be reached only through their mother tongue, one of the indigenous languages of the country, or an interpreter.

Another interesting experience was the work she sometimes did in her foster mother's store. There she learned the rudiments of business, especially how to cater to the desires of customers. She delighted in telling how she and her foster mother made adjustments to various merchandise that moved too slowly off the shelves, for example, adding flowers to hats or changing flowers or bands on hats which customers did not seem to like. This exercise provided opportunities for her to apply the knowledge she was acquiring in sewing and helped to develop in her a taste for the high fashions of the day.

Yet another influence to which she was exposed was music. She learned to play the organ and to sing and sharpened these skills as she participated in the life of the First Baptist Church in Edina to which her foster mother belonged and where she attended. In this Church, she was organist for a period. She also sang in the Choir. As I remember, she had a beautiful soprano voice and the words of any song she sang came forth with clarity and distinctness. For her, clear enunciation of the words of a song was most important. One of the ways she rated a singer was how well the text of what was sung could be understood by the audience.

The center of her informal education was the home, under the capable guidance of her foster mother. The overriding value she imbibed was reverence for God. Next, she learned the importance of the family and what it meant to be part of a family. Other important things she learned were how to manage a home, the domestic arts of cooking and sewing and hospitality to strangers and other visitors to the home. Work was an essential part of living and she learned to appreciate the dignity in labor and develop an appropriate attitude to work. Through these experiences and especially the love and warmth of her foster mother, she developed a sense of self and worth; the virtues of honesty and integrity; and a genuine love and respect for people, regardless of their circumstance or station in life.

Her formal education which, with these influences, gave her a well-rounded education in her childhood and youth was obtained at Brierly Memorial, an Episcopal school for girls in Harper, Cape Palmas. It seems she entered this school around the time it was reopened in 1898, in newly rebuilt quarters, named for Mrs. Maria Brierly, a missionary who worked for 15 years for the Episcopal Mission in Cape Mount, pioneering in the education of girls in that region of Liberia and dying there in 1895.[8]   The school housed in Brierly Memorial Hall resulted from the consolidation in 1883 of the Boarding School for Native Girls, originally established at Cavalla in the interior of Cape Palmas and later transferred to Harper and the Orphan Asylum, initially opened at Harper, on the Cape, in April, 1855.

The better known of the two schools, the Orphan Asylum, was founded during the Episcopacy of Bishop John Payne, about five years after the Protestant Episcopal Mission opened a high school at Mount Vaughn, Cape Palmas, for the male children of settlers. It was the earliest school for girls in the Cape Palmas region. This was also the case for the rest of Liberia for the period following the declaration of independence in 1847. The Orphan Asylum preceded by more than a half century the Episcopal schools for girls, Bromley Mission, St. Paul River and Bethany Mission, Robertsport, Cape Mount. Visualized by Bishop Payne, it was planned as:

An institution specifically set apart for female orphans where they might have not only a Christian home, but also Christian training and nurture and so prepare them for future usefulness in the mission both as wives and mothers and, if possible, as co-laborers in the work of the Mission.[9]

The goals of the school and its course of study suggest that its standards were high. From the course of study, we learn that the school began with four classes. The fourth, apparently devoted to beginners, concentrated on the alphabet "on cards and blocks." The third class dealt with Spelling and Reading. The academic subjects of the second class were: "Study Elements of Geography, with Globe and Maps (out line): Grammar, Spelling and Defining, First Book of History, Natural Philosophy for children, Writing and Rudiments of Arithmetic." The academic subjects for the first class were "History, Geography, Scholar's Companion, Arithmetic, writing and Composition," also "Grammar, Elements of Physiology and Botany."[10]

The morning period of the school, which convened Monday to Friday for three hours and 15 minutes (9:15 to 12:30), was devoted to academic subjects. There was an afternoon session three afternoons a week, (Wednesday through Friday) which was a sewing school. The other two afternoons, the matron taught the girls to wash and iron their clothes.

For religious development, the girls were required to attend morning and evening prayers daily. They also attended Church each Sunday morning and Sunday School each Sunday afternoon at St. Mark Episcopal Church, Harper, Cape Palmas. Early during Victoria's studies at Brierly Memorial, she was baptized at St. Mark. In 1899, she was also confirmed at St. Mark. The Bishop officiating at her confirmation was Bishop Samuel David Ferguson, the first Liberian to become Bishop of the Protestant Episcopal Church in Liberia.

Initially in charge of the institution were Rev. H. R. Scott and his wife, Mrs. Anna Scott. On July 21, 1855, shortly after the founding of the institution, Mrs. Scott wrote:

> The Orphan Asylum is highly esteemed by the people of this community, most of whom are awake to the great importance of education and anxious to obtain its inestimable privileges for their children.[11]

The building that housed the institution, strategically situated on the promontory of Cape Palmas, caught the eye of passersby and was described as a "moral lighthouse."[12] It was in a salubrious location and had a commanding view of the ocean and its picturesque vistas. Thus, it also served as a place of rest and recuperation for missionaries and other foreign workers in the Cape Palmas area and along the nearby coast.

The record on the consolidated institution is rather sparse. However, in 1896, 13 years after the consolidation, the Orphan Asylum and Girls School had an enrollment of 91-75 boarders and 16 day scholars. It had a lower department of "68 "native" African boarding scholars and 10 day pupils" and a higher department of "six aboriginal and one American-Liberian boarding beneficiaries and six American-Liberian day scholars. ..."[13]

Studies in the lower department consisted of "the Scriptures, first, second and third American Educational Readers, Smith's English Grammar, Spelling, Arithmetic and Writing." The studies of the upper department were: the Holy Scriptures, the new American fifth Reader, the Fourth American Educational Reader, Cornell's Geography, Arithmetic, Smith's Speller and definer and Conklin's practical lessons in language and writing.[14]

Brierly Memorial, as the school was known from 1898, operated until 1927 when it closed for "reorganization and never reopened."[15]

Returning to Victoria's informal education, other noteworthy influences were those which came with adulthood and followed her marriage and return to Monrovia to live. A major one of these was her reconnection with Vai society and culture, highlighted by traditional marriage rites. While her parents were aware of where she was for most of the time she was in Edina and had kept a link with her, circumstances such as distance and poor transportation facilities had hindered their interaction with her. In Monrovia, she was nearer and could be more easily reached by her family of consanguinity. The necessary interaction occurred.

Also important in this reconnection was the reunion with her mother and Pai. Her father died before her return to Monrovia. Pai had been reared according to Vai customs, amidst informal indigenous influences and the formal initiation rites school of the Vais for girls, the Sande. Also, in keeping with the Vai custom of the early betrothal and marriage of girls (as was the custom for other indigenous ethnic groups in Liberia), Pai was married and had begun having her children. She had a total of 10 children - five boys and five girls, two of whom died in infancy. Victoria started having children later that year and had a total of five - four boys and myself, referred to by her relatives as a musu dondo (one girl). Their relationship became cemented and, although Victoria could not be fully reintegrated into Vai society, having missed initiation into the Sande, many opportunities opened over time for her to become familiar with Vai customs and for Pai to share with her in Monrovia the events of joy and sadness which occurred in her life.

Figuring prominently in her reconnection with and reeducation to Vai society and culture was her Uncle, Chief Varney Marbue of Jondu. Her Uncle Varney Marbue ensured that she retained her roots in Vai society and culture in various ways. He told her stories of the Kiazolu clan and its significance in Vai culture and society, thereby reinforcing the little knowledge she had acquired of the clan as a child. He helped her to get to know her consanguinal relatives and strengthened her kinship ties. Also, he saw to it that she regained fluency in Vai. One way was by sending young Vai boys to her home for short periods, which made her use Vai in English-speaking Monrovia, as these children could not speak English. He expressed concern, as she mentioned to us on several occasions, that she spoke "classical Vai," that is, Vai that was not mixed with the English words that were creeping into the Vai language and also into other Liberian languages. One indication of his impact on her and her husband and their affection for him was the fact that they gave their fourth son one of his names, Marbue.[16] The name, Marbue, is perpetuated through two succeeding generations; my last child, Byrd Arthur Marbue Brown, and his first child, Joel Marbue Brown.

Other relatives who contributed to her readjustment to Vai culture were Chief Boima Njoh of Vai Town, situated partly on the Mesurado River between Stockton Creek and the Atlantic Ocean, across from Monrovia and Zuke Kandakai, who became well known for the assistance he gave in later years to Professor Klingenheben of Hamburg University in his research and study of the Vai language and culture. They also figured strongly in the lives of her children- my siblings and myself.

On Sundays, our father often took us out walking and visiting in and around Monrovia and sometimes to Vai Town where Cousin Boima Njoh and other relatives of our mother lived. The trips to Vai Town had to be made by canoe, as this was prior to the construction in 1944 of the first bridge that joined Bushrod Island, on which Vai Town is located and Monrovia. Our parents placed a premium on these visits, for it was not simple to travel with a bunch of children across the Mesurado River by canoe, the prevailing mode of travel at the time between Vai Town and Monrovia. The trips were like adventure. However, they were enjoyable and paid dividends in terms of family relationships and immersion in Vai culture. In addition, we learned to recognize different types of canoes and know which were safest. We also learned how to sit in a canoe to keep it in balance, minimizing its chances of capsizing.

My mother's cousin, Fahnwullu, the link with her family and ethnic group from her years as a child in Edina, remained a vital part of her life until his death. He continued to live on through the close ties she maintained with his children, George, Augustus Feweh and Lydia Zoe.

Feweh has stated that among Fahnwullu's children that kinship was experienced as a "spiritual relationship." He characterized it as "stronger than a blood kinship." And he noted: Our affection for her derived from her deep feeling for the Kiazolu people and her caring love for them.

The other major influence in my mother's informal education was my father. As they quite naturally became immersed in the life and work of each other after their marriage, he sought her opinion on the speeches he was called on to make from time to time and the documents he produced in connection with his work. Accordingly, she did much reading and exchanging of ideas and views with him and extended her reading to areas of general knowledge and pleasure as well. As he traveled, especially during the early 1930s to Geneva, Switzerland, in defense of his country at the League of Nations, her world broadened as she vicariously shared with him the experiences of his travels in Europe and his work at the League. Meanwhile, her background continued to be a source of fascination for him. He maintained an interest in the Vai language, which he learned to speak and Vai customs, which he began to study early in their marriage as he delved into her background. The story which he wrote, based on the information he obtained, formed the basis more than 50 years later and 21 years after his death, for The Liberia Official Gazette, vol. xlix, No. 4, April 23, 1970, released by the Government of Liberia at the time of her death in April, 1970, and for subsequent biographical accounts of her.

CHAPTER 3

Chosen to Become a Bride

Mechlin House, home of the Cheeseman family, was a natural attraction for visitors from Bassa County as well as from Monrovia and other places outside of the County. Among those who were visitors to the home in 1907 and the years following in connection with his work of assisting in the prosecution of criminal cases in Bassa County, was Louis Arthur Grimes, then County Attorney for Montserrado County.[17]

Louis' visits to the home brought him in contact with a charming young person whom he could not resist. Victoria, one of the foster daughters of Mary Ann Cheeseman, was medium height, brown-skinned and simply beautiful. She had medium length black hair and bright eyes. Intelligent and lively, she was a good conversationalist. She was also industrious and pleasant. The normal activities in the home in which she was involved included hospitality to visitors. On Louis' visits to their home, she exhibited the warmth and vibrancy characteristic of her. She soon realized that she had captured his eye and his heart. The advances made by him struck a responsive chord in her. The mutual feelings began to blossom into a relationship of love.

Louis was an eligible bachelor. A descendant of the Barclay family, both of his parents immigrated to Liberia from Barbados, West Indies. His mother, Ella Mai Gilbert Barclay, was the last of the 12 children of her parents, Anthony Barclay and Sarah Ann Barclay. She came to Liberia in May, 1865, with her parents and 10 siblings - seven sisters and three brothers - when she was not quite nine years old.[18] They were part of the famous West Indian immigration of 346 persons, led by her father, the only immigration from the West Indies to Liberia in the 19th century.[19]

Louis' father, Henry Waldron Grimes, immigrated to Liberia as an adult in the 1870s after having spent a brief period in the United States. His parents were married in Monrovia and Louis, their first child, was born on Sept. 8, 1883. Their only other child, Florence Mai Isabel, was born March 26. 1885. Louis was nearly 11 and Mai nine, when their father died, so they were largely reared by their mother, with the assistance of the older brother next to her in age, Arthur Barclay and the reinforcement of a closely knit Barclay family.

When Louis began visiting Edina, he had received a Bachelor's degree from Liberia College (now University of Liberia) in the class of 1903; was a promising young lawyer; and had entered Government service. He was serving simultaneously as County Attorney for Montserrado County, a position to which he was appointed in 1907 and City Solicitor for the Municipal Government of the City of Monrovia. Moreover, he was a Grimes and to the widow of President Cheeseman, the Grimes name was not strange. His father, who died on June 4, 1894, had served in Cheeseman's Cabinet as Attorney General from January, 1894, until his death, a period of about five months.

The love that was sparked when Louis met Victoria was the driving force which led him to ask for her hand in marriage, but there were other factors which propelled the development of their relationship. He was impressed by her affability, intelligence, industriousness and home management skills. Also, they had some common interests, among them, a love of people and a love of music. Regarding the latter, both of them were using their talents in music in similar ways; she, singing in the Choir and playing the organ for the First Baptist Church of Edina, and he, serving as Choir Master for the Junior Choir of Trinity Memorial Church (now Trinity Cathedral) in Monrovia. They were also using this talent in activities in their respective communities.

Added to these was the fact that Louis wanted to marry someone of indigenous background. Years earlier, his Uncle Arthur married across ethnic lines, establishing a precedent for the family. After the death of his first wife, Mary Marshall Barclay, he married Jane Seton Davis Lomax, a Grebo woman, who had been twice widowed, having lost her first husband, William McCall Davis, and her second husband, Thomas C. Lomax.

Moreover, while Louis was a student at Liberia College, he studied under Dr. Edward Wilmot Blyden who by then had grown to appreciate African customs and values and had communicated this sense of appreciation to his students. On several occasions, he mentioned to us that Blyden had advocated intermarriage between people of settler stock and those of indigenous stock. Blyden believed that such marriages, still rare at that time, would contribute to better relations between the two groups of people in the country. Louis was aware that a match between him and Victoria would be a step in this direction.[20] She was a prize.

Soon, the news began to spread that Louis was looking for a bride, not in Monrovia as was expected, but in Edina and that his choice was Victoria. This did not set well with Monrovians, who were then mainly of settler stock and generally felt themselves superior to the other people of the country. Their prejudice was against people of indigenous stock (aka the "country people"), settlers and recaptives who found home along the St. Paul River (aka the "up-river people"), people (aka the "coast people") in the counties other than Montserrado, then all coastal. Victoria was of indigenous stock and had been reared in Grand Bassa County, a coastal County - two strikes. Why would he decide to choose her? Why was his choice "Mrs. Cheeseman's Vai girl," as they tried to put it derogatively? What about the eligible maidens in Monrovia, especially the young ladies who were attending college and those who were among the handful of women who had recently completed college and earned the distinction of being the first women in the country to attain college degrees?

Louis was not moved by these negative inquiries. He was in love and he believed that Victoria would make him a good wife. Victoria did not pay any attention to these prejudices either. She was proud of her indigenous roots and proud of her upbringing. Little did it matter to her how her relationship to her foster mother was characterized. For her, she was Mary Ann Cheeseman's daughter and Mary Ann Cheeseman was her mother. She was in love and she knew she merited Louis' hand. Years after her marriage, when she spoke about the prejudices which emerged when Louis began to focus his attention on her, she would smile and say her answer at the time to those putting the negative questions was the private thought, "I'll show them."

For Louis, there was no need for hesitation. He knew what he wanted. He took a step forward by requesting his Uncle Arthur, whose inauguration as President for a third term was January, 1908, to add a personal note to the formal invitation extended Victoria's foster mother to attend the inauguration. His hope was that she would make the trip to Monrovia and have Victoria accompany her. This was exactly what happened and Louis used the opportunity to introduce Victoria to his family. Some months later, he requested her hand in marriage. She consented and her foster mother gave them her blessings.

CHAPTER 4

Wedding Bells and a *Musu Tombo*

Dec. 10, 1911, was a special day in the city of Edina. Wedding bells rang and Victoria Elizabeth Cheeseman was joined in Holy Wedlock to Louis Arthur Grimes in St. Luke Episcopal Church in that city. The officiating clergy was Rev. F. Africanus K. Russell, a Clergyman of the Episcopal Church and a personal friend of Louis. The ritual was that of the Book of Common Prayer of the Protestant Episcopal Church. Louis' first cousin whom he had grown up close to, Anthony Barclay - son of his Uncle Arthur - was the best man and Victoria's close friend, Eliza Rae Jackson, was the maid of honor. Also participating in the ceremony with Louis was another first cousin to whom he had grown close and a classmate of his at Liberia College, Edwin James Barclay (nickname Eddie).[21] The wedding reception was held at Mechlin House.

What joy for Victoria's foster mother who had spent 15 years nurturing this child whom it seems God had sent her to help dry the tears she was shedding when she lost the last surviving of her own children! Victoria had conducted herself as was expected and, by her marriage, was making her foster mother proud.

In Liberia at the time, marriage was the most important milestone in the life of a girl. It was a premium expectation for a girl and was to take place as close to her reaching adulthood as possible. This was true in the Liberian indigenous societies as well as in Liberian "sophisticated society." In the former, adulthood was marked by the "coming out" of the Sande or similar indigenous society, that is, soon after puberty and in the latter, the majority age of 18. Chastity until marriage was required. A girl who remained a virgin until marriage bestowed pride on her family. Her wedding was accordingly celebrated as a big, public event, a festive occasion which began with a church ceremony and ended with a reception.

Victoria, then 22 years old, was being married to a promising young man. She would go off to establish her own home, but would always remain a part of her foster mother's heart and life - "My dear child," as she affectionately greeted her when she wrote to her after she was married and settled in Monrovia. And her foster mother and her family would always hold a special place in her heart and life. Through her, close ties had already been established between the Cheeseman family and the Kiazolu clan. By this marriage, both the Cheeseman family and the Kiazolu clan were being united with the Barclay family.

For the people of Edina, it was a big day in their city. Victoria, affectionately called "Sis Vic" by many of them, had grown up in their city. A lively and warm person, she had been a part of their lives in many different ways. She had played for the First Baptist Church, made dresses for the leading ladies of their city, and had in other ways been useful and helpful in their community. They too were proud of her and wanted to share in the joy of her special day. They pulled out their best clothes and did just that.

The wedding was referred to in The Liberia Official Gazette, released at the time of Victoria's death, as "fashionable." The occasion was indeed festive, one of pomp. A former first lady of the nation - President Cheeseman's widow - and a prominent citizen in her own right was marrying off her daughter. There was, however, more to the occasion than glamour. Underlying the festivity was the spiritual commitment of two persons deeply in love with each other, united under God in a Christian marriage ceremony. God blessed the marriage and they lived together happily until they were separated by Louis' death on Dec. 14, 1948 - four days after their 37th wedding anniversary.

The celebration of Louis' marriage to Victoria did not end in Edina, where she was nurtured. Jondu, Gawula Chiefdom, Cape Mount, her place of birth, would have its day also. She was a product of both. It was an inter-ethnic war that, in the first place, took her away from her consanguinal relatives. They could hardly wait for the day when the child who left them would return to them a married woman!

Louis and Victoria were hardly settled in Monrovia when contact was established with her people and preparations were begun for traditional marriage rites to be held in Jondu. According to Vai custom, a *musu tombo* (wedding feast) signified pre-marital chastity and had to be arranged and expenses borne by the bride's people.[22]   The Kiazolu clan was thus given the opportunity to celebrate and thereby experience the pride and joy which, according to their customs, marrying off a young virgin bestows upon her family.

The festive occasion was held in February, 1912, two months after the wedding ceremony in Edina. It was a celebration befitting a Ruling House of the Vais! Masked figures, dancers, singers and musical ensembles led the people of Jondu, other parts of Gawula and the Vai country and Monrovia in much singing and dancing to honor a daughter who remembered Jondu. Indeed, the saying was in a way validated, that if anything good comes to someone from Jondu, that person returns to Jondu. It is unfortunate that Victoria could not be physically present for such a historic occasion. She was in the early stage of her first pregnancy, suffering the illness and discomfort which she experienced throughout the pregnancy and also in all subsequent pregnancies. However, Louis was there for himself and her. Eddie Barclay participated with him in this ceremony as in that held earlier in Edina.

The *musu tombo* formally sealed the tie which had already been made between the Kiazolu clan and the Barclay family according to the customs of the Kiazolus, giving the relationship real significance for the clan. The occasion was memorable in the life of the couple and their families and provided an interesting signal in settler-indigenous relations.

CHAPTER 5

Carving a Niche in Monrovia

What would life in Monrovia be like for Victoria? Could she overcome the prejudice of Monrovians against her and the jealousy of those who felt Louis should have selected one of his hometown girls?

She and Louis arrived in Monrovia from Edina to a warm welcome from his family. For his close relatives, his choice of a wife was theirs. Already 28 at the time of his marriage, his relatives were happy to see him married. They welcomed Victoria into the family.

Home for the couple for the first year was the Barclay family home on Broad Street at Center Street, opposite Providence Baptist Church, where his mother and her older sister, Malvina, lived. Louis was having his own home built at the other end of Broad Street, commonly called Snapper Hill, but it was not yet completed. The warmth of welcome Victoria received, needless to say, was very pleasing to her. On several occasions, she remarked that on their arrival to what would be home for them for a while, Louis' mother and his Aunt Malvina (Aunt Mal), "folded her into their arms," and she decided that she would remain in their fold for the rest of her life. And that she did. The other of this trio of older Barclays, Louis' Uncle Arthur and his wife, Florence, joined in giving Victoria a warm welcome. Louis' only sibling, Mai, then already married to Richard Stanley Wiles and with her own home and two small children (Lducia and Stanley), also welcomed Victoria. A similarly warm welcome was accorded Victoria by those first cousins of Louis who lived in Monrovia: Eddie Barclay and his wife, Euphemia (nickname Phemie); Anthony Barclay, later married to Sarah Raynes; Elizabeth Barclay (nickname Lizzie), later Mrs. Reginald Sherman; and Mary Barclay, later Mrs. Stanley Padmore.[23]

Victoria fitted easily into the circle of the immediate family. The difference in age between her and Mai, Phemie, Lizzie, Mary and Sarah, who joined the family in April, 1917, was small. She was a little younger than Mai and Phemie and a little older than Lizzie, Mary and Sarah. Their interests were similar, they, coming from the background of the élite Monrovia society and she, from the élite society of Edina, which at the time was not much different from Monrovia in significance. Moreover, within the first 10 years of Victoria's marriage to Louis, they were all young wives. Practically all of them were having and rearing their small children, in reality, ushering in a new generation of Barclays-the fourth in Liberia. Living for the most part in close proximity to one another, they shared the traditions of the Barclay family. Their tie to their Aunt Mal, then the oldest living of the 11 Barclay children who immigrated to Liberia with their parents, was strong. It brought them together in regular visits to her home which, over time, became regular Sunday afternoon visits to her by all members of the family in the Monrovia area. There, three generations of Barclays met and shared their history, memories of their past, their joys and hopes, their concerns and sorrows. There they all relaxed and enjoyed the amenities of the home and the views of buildings and events in Monrovia which its central location afforded. There they partook of fruits from the yard and other food, especially the "sweet bread" their Aunt Mal, even when she reached her 90s, delighted in making and seeing the grown-ups as well as the children enjoy eating. Among the many happy memories of my childhood were the Sunday visits our family made to Aunt Mal.

A warm atmosphere was created by the family right from the start and it was a source of strength as Victoria settled to provide her husband love and companionship and meet his daily needs through the home. This was a very important first step in her adjustment to Monrovia. She was given her rightful place in the family and the members of the family found her warm and responsive to them. Married life was off to a pleasant start, with the love and support of Louis' closest relatives, never mind those Monrovians who, because of prejudice, criticized his decision to make her his wife.

Victoria had hardly arrived in Monrovia when she discovered that she was not only a wife but also an expectant mother. Although she was a strong person who rarely became ill through much of her life, this was a difficult time, for in this pregnancy, as in all succeeding ones, she suffered the discomfort of nausea and vomiting, not merely for the usual approximately two months of morning sickness, but throughout the pregnancy. She naturally was very much wrapped up in herself. But, pregnancy carries with it the joyful expectancy of a new life and for Victoria, the happy day was Sept. 5, 1912. On that day, she delivered their first, a baby boy, who was named Louis Arthur after his father and called Arthur. What joy and blessing! There was also the added thrill, for she, like women in Liberian "sophisticated society" at that time, thought it special to have their first child within the first year of their marriage. This meant that the woman was fertile and, at the time, young wives were literally obsessed about being fertile. After all, reproduction was then central to marriage in Liberia - in fact, considered practically the be-all and end-all of marriage. Children were expected to begin arriving soon after marriage. If a marriage did not yield children, people, for the most part, felt something was wrong and the tendency was to place the blame on the woman. Even in my day, I remember the smile that lighted my mother's face each time she spoke of Arthur's arrival nine months after she and my father were married.

A young mother shortly after marriage, Victoria experienced all the demands on her time that a baby brings and the joys of motherhood. Indeed, a baby provides the opportunity of seeing the divine hand, God's Hand, at work in the world and of marveling at the miracle of life. Victoria experienced this time of reflection, wonder and joy as she watched from one day to the next and saw her child grow and develop - hold up his head, respond to sounds, smile, crawl, walk and talk. Like other young mothers, she enjoyed sharing the news of her child's development and especially, of comparing notes with young mothers she got to meet, regarding his development and that of their babies. Soon, she was in the circle of young mothers in the environs of her home and within a fair radius of the community. Like these mothers, she enjoyed playing with and dressing up her baby. Skilled in sewing, she began making clothes and bonnets for him. Soon, her handiwork attracted attention in this place where ready-made clothing was not easily obtained. Her service was sought to make bonnets and clothes for other babies and more and more her handiwork was admired. She began to be called upon by an increasing number of persons and she soon found herself playing an important role in the community in the course of her day-to-day activities. Her circle of admirers and friends gradually began to widen.

In the meantime, on Dec. 31, 1912, she and Louis, with little Arthur, moved into the three-story frame house, which Louis was having built. Although it was not completed, it was in a livable condition. Louis arranged the move then, as neither of them wished to move in 1913, no doubt because 13 was then, as it sometimes is now, associated with bad luck.

Victoria had enjoyed the period they shared the home with her mother-in-law, but every wife welcomes her own home and the opportunity of putting her stamp on the home. Victoria was no exception. Her new home was a challenge and a joy. She set about to manage it and make it cozy and inviting, characteristics it would always have. Meanwhile, their second child, another boy, arrived, March 21, 1914, and she had additional responsibilities as a mother. He was named Henry Waldron after his paternal grandfather and called Henry.

In those days, a husband was the center of the home, and everything revolved around him. He was considered the breadwinner. Men earned their daily bread usually through work outside of the home but sometimes from private offices and workshops run from their homes. For women, their forté was the home.

Victoria felt strongly about the importance of the home and her role as wife and mother in it. She catered to the needs of her husband, cooked and served delicious meals and took care of their children. She was also involved in planting fruits and the small garden which was a part of practically every home in Monrovia at that time. Such gardens contained vegetables to be used in meals for the family and medicinal plants, such as catnip, fever tea and pigeon peas, which provided the herbal remedies many used since medical doctors were rare and folk medicine was the vogue. Her cultivation efforts also included a small flower garden. Snapper Hill was a rocky area, so none of this planting activity was easy.

As for Louis, he had qualified as a Counsellor-at-Law on Jan. 16, 1911, which meant he could practice not only in the Lower Courts but also before the Supreme Court. He wanted to concentrate on private law practice and the end of the administration of President Arthur Barclay-December 1911-seemed a good time to end his service with Government. This meant that he would not be serving in the upcoming administration of President Daniel Edward Howard, and he did not wish to. It seemed also a good time to get married and begin a new period in his life. Accordingly, he married on Dec. 10, 1911 and resigned the position he held in Government at the end of December, 1911.

Thus, Victoria literally began her married life as Louis established a private law practice at the beginning of 1912. Gradually, his practice grew, no doubt because he was known to accept cases only when he felt his clients had been wronged and stood a chance of winning and also because he settled as much as possible out of court. His clients included people from both settler and indigenous backgrounds and from all walks of life.

Among the cases he argued before the Supreme Court during the early years of his practice, my brother, Rudolph, drew my attention to one which can be described as landmark. It dealt with a major problem in the integration process in the country, a matter about which Louis' marriage made him increasingly sensitive. The issue in question related to the political subdivision of the country into counties and provinces, that portion beyond the 40-mile limit of the counties, and then referred to as the "hinterland," placed under the authority of the Interior Department. His clients, Ballah Karmo and Worhn Beh, were contesting their imprisonment by the Secretary of the Interior and the Officer Commanding the Frontier Force and the constitutionality of the Act of the Legislature approved Oct. 13, 1914, which gave the Interior Department the authority for such action as had been taken against them.[24] They felt that dividing the country in this way resulted in inequities in administering the country, favoring those of settler stock, who resided mainly in the five counties and discriminating against those of indigenous stock, the majority of whom resided in the three Provinces,[25] the "hinterland."

The Supreme Court, then headed by Chief Justice J. J. Dossen,[26] ruled in favor of his clients, declaring the Legislative Act of Oct. 13, 1914 unconstitutional. Several decades would elapse, however, before this decision would be brought to the forefront by President William V. S. Tubman. It proved to be a motivator for and propelled his initiative for restructuring the country in 1962. He established a Commission to deal with this matter and the result of their work was the division of the country into nine counties, providing equal access and rights for all the people of the country.

With Louis in private law practice, their home doubled up as a Law Office where he took care of clients and accepted students as apprentices, the apprenticeship system being, at the time, the only means of training in Liberia to become a lawyer. Thus, their home was open to more than the normal movement of people for a home and Victoria had to manage the home to take care of this circumstance and to assist her husband as best as she could. In addition to her regular duties, she extended courtesies to those who sought her husband's service, whenever needed. There were people from various walks of life, many times troubled, consulting her husband to seek redress for them and young adults preparing for a career in law who came as apprentices. While she was not directly involved in the Office, there was interaction with some of this diverse group of people. The number of people in Monrovia who got to know her increased accordingly.

Another area in which Victoria made herself felt was the Church. When she settled in Monrovia with Louis, she became a member of his Church, Trinity Memorial Church (now Trinity Cathedral). Although her foster mother was a Baptist and she had attended, served as organist and sung in the Choir in the First Baptist Church in Edina, she was no stranger to the Episcopal Church. It was in an Episcopal Church that she had been baptized and confirmed (St. Mark Episcopal Church, Harper, Cape Palmas) and married (St. Luke Episcopal Church, Edina, Grand Bassa). Moreover, there were the same basic Christian teachings in these two denominations.

Victoria regularly attended worship services with Louis and became involved in the work of Trinity, mainly as a Sunday school teacher and as a member of the organization of women, called the Women's Auxiliary at the time and later, Episcopal Church Women (ECW). The small children and youth of the Church came under her instruction and her influence. She also shared with a number of other women in the various responsibilities they had for the work of the Church. The time was an interesting and challenging one, as Trinity assumed full responsibility for its operation and finance in 1916. The first Church in the Missionary Diocese of the Protestant Episcopal Church in Liberia to assume such responsibility, this occurred almost coincidental in time with the move of Victoria and Louis to their home which was situated about a couple of blocks from Trinity.

Victoria was also involved in the life of the community. Snapper Hill was a relatively new section of Monrovia. The people who lived there ensured that the area was maintained for health, safety and aesthetic reasons. There was a tacit agreement among them that each family would not merely keep in shape their family property - grass trimmed and free of trash - but also the surrounding areas. As yet, the Municipality and the Government had not taken on such responsibility. There were no available funds. The women oversaw this work and Victoria was active in their endeavors. There were also social and cultural activities in the community in which she participated. For example, occasionally, groups of couples would gather in the home of a couple and would have as part of the gathering a time for reciting, singing and playing the piano and other musical instruments. Victoria made her contribution to such activities, as did Louis. She also performed in the cantatas and concerts which were held in the public halls to mark special occasions.

In fact, she took advantage of opportunities to use her talents for the good of her family, her Church and her community. Meanwhile, through interaction with her family of consanguinity, she strengthened her links with the family and learned to understand and appreciate deeply the "royal" clan of the Vais from which she sprang. Speaking Vai with her people, English, most of the time and Bassa, as the occasion warranted, she conversed in all three, moving with ease from one to the other, enjoying people, buying from petty traders or doing other business-all in the course of day-to-day living.

Their marriage was off to a good start and she was enjoying it, not oblivious to how rare intermarriage between people of settler and indigenous stock was at that time and how her own marriage was sending signals of the potentials such intermarriages could have.

CHAPTER 6

Wife and Mother in a Liberian Extended Family

Louis was the center of Victoria's life. She was his delight. Daily they grew closer to each other as they shared and enjoyed each other's love and companionship. She was very attentive to him and he grew dependent on her as she did on him, perhaps he more so. The birth of each child added to their joy and together they spent much time and thought in the upbringing of their children. Over time, the children of relatives, friends and admirers were brought into the family. Louis and Victoria also devoted time and attention to rearing them and they too contributed to the family's happiness.

Within the first three years of their marriage, there were two little boys, Arthur and Henry and a home of their own. Louis was in work that brought him satisfaction, a comfortable income and flexibility that the alternative of government service did not allow at that time. Victoria was happily settling into her role of wife and mother. All was going well with them. Soon, however, they had to deal with the challenges of difficult and sad times.

First, there was the outbreak of World War I on Aug. 12, 1914. The war triggered a feeling of insecurity in the country, especially after Monrovia was bombarded in 1917 by a German submarine in an attempt to destroy the French wireless station in Monrovia which the Government had refused to close, despite demands from the Germans. Liberia had declared neutrality in the War and the station was the main link with the outside world, but these facts carried no weight with the Germans. They were at war with the nations which had banded themselves together as the Allies and France was a major one of those nations.

The second problem with which Louis and Victoria had to deal was the economic hardship which the country faced, a situation which became aggravated when, later in 1917; Liberia declared war on the side of the Allies. At the time, Germany was Liberia's main trading partner.

During this period, the couple had two sad experiences. The first was the death of Victoria's foster mother. She and Louis were overwhelmed with sadness when they received word of her death, especially as they learned that she had expressed the wish to have Victoria with her during her illness. She must have wondered when she did not see her.

Unfortunately, it was some time after her foster mother had died and was buried before they received the news. Victoria could not even attend the funeral. How she wished that she could have been with her foster mother to show her affection and provide her comfort at a time she needed her! Every time she thought about what had happened, she was saddened, never mind that it was all beyond her control. Her grief was deep and so was Louis'. Sometimes, she wondered whether slowness of communication was the actual cause of the delayed message or whether it was deliberate. She suspected that a close relative of her foster mother, jealous of the close relationship she had with her, had engineered the delay of the message to prevent her from responding to her foster mother's desire to have her around her in her final days. That relative felt that her absence would prevent her foster mother sharing her precious possessions with her and providing her any information regarding disposal of her property.

As if her foster mother's death was not hard enough, another blow befell Louis and her. This time, the person affected was their little son, Arthur. He became ill with black water fever and despite the fact that everything that was medically possible was done, he did not recover. On Dec. 1, 1919, almost three months after his seventh birthday, he died.

It is hard to lose any loved one, but to lose one's child is heartrending! Louis and Victoria were stricken with grief beyond words. They had not dreamed they would have to "pay ground," that is, bury a child, the meaning this common Liberian expression conveyed. Growing no doubt out of the high infant mortality situation then existing in the country, the expression implied that the ground had a claim against every couple. Burying a child was simply settling the claim or debt, for each couple was expected to bury one child or more. This resignation was no comfort for Louis and Victoria. Their loss was a cold reality that they had to face.

Associated with the death of Arthur were two unusual occurrences. First, Victoria had a premonition of his death. During his illness, she had a dream in which she saw her foster mother standing over her and looking pityingly at her. Then, she took Arthur by the hand and led him away. It seemed her foster mother was assuring her that all would be well with him. A day or two thereafter, Arthur died. This dream was to recur later in her life, with another of her children in the picture.

Second, Ella, the third child of Mai and Richard, displayed considerable emotion and grief. The same age as Arthur, the two were playmates and very close. Shortly after Arthur died, Ella became ill. To the family's surprise, she expressed that she wanted to be with Arthur. It was not long after that she too died, leaving her parents grief-stricken and bringing sadness to the rest of the family. The two were buried beside each other in the Grimes' plot in the Palm Grove Cemetery, Center Street, Monrovia. For the family, the loss of two small children at practically the same time was overwhelming. It took time to accept the loss and adjust to it. For Louis and Victoria, it took even more time to get over the pain of the deaths of three close ones, Arthur especially and to have as a precious part of their lives the memory of these three loved ones. They faced the decade of the 1920s with hope for a return of happy times. Such times came with two major sets of events: (1) Victoria's return to childbearing, which yielded a second set of children, three in number and, (2) Louis' career change.

With reference to the first of these changes, Victoria's third pregnancy had ended in a miscarriage in 1915 and she had had to take a rest from childbearing. In early 1923, she welcomed becoming pregnant again. On Oct. 31 of that year, she delivered their third child, another boy. They named him Joseph Rudolph and called him on a regular basis Rudolph - Joseph, after Victoria's foster father and Rudolph, after two of Louis' European friends, the baron, Rudolph Lehman and the Hungarian doctor, Rudolph Fuszek, both of whom had ties to Liberia through their work for the country. Henry, who had begun life as little brother and for almost four years had been an only child, was now in the position of big brother. Two other children soon followed, accentuating that place for him.

I was the first of these two children-the fourth child and my parents' long hoped for girl! I was born on Oct. 27, 1926. My father's initial wish was for me to be named after my mother. She, however, was desirous of having me named Mary Ann after her foster mother, who meant a whole lot to her. That was fine with my father, except that he did not like the name, Ann. Accordingly, he sought a compromise - agreeing to the name, Mary, but dropping the Ann and adding instead Antoinette Hope, after Antoinette Hope Barclay, the oldest sibling of his mother. A teacher at a time in Liberia where a good education was hard to come by, she had taught him, her other nephews and her nieces, who were living in Monrovia, through primary school. All of them had gone on successfully in their studies. He too wanted to take the opportunity to honor someone who had made a significant impact on his life. The name my parents agreed to was Mary Antoinette Hope, calling me on a regular basis by the first two names, Mary Antoinette.

The last of this second set of children, the youngest of us and another boy, arrived Aug. 3, 1928. He was named Ernest Marbue after a paternal and a maternal granduncle and called Marbue.

Aunty Mai, my father's sister who had several children about the same time my mother was having children, told of how her brother often jokingly reminded them, with each respective pregnancy, of the Biblical saying: "Increase, multiply and replenish the Earth." (Genesis 9:1)

According to him, increase meant up to two children; multiply, three to four; and replenish, five and upwards. Well, when Marbue was born, the joke was on him. He confessed to Aunty Mai one day that he was getting tired of increasing, multiplying and replenishing the Earth. His girl had given him the spunk to continue, but the fourth boy had convinced him that boys were what he and my mother could expect. He was calling it quits.

During this period, the family of my parents more than doubled. Having lost Arthur, they now had four children. Meanwhile, the family was also growing by other than natural accessions. Ever since the young Vai boys began coming from Uncle Varney shortly after my mother's marriage to help her regain fluency in Vai, the home was open to other than their own children. These boys were transient, but by the time of Arthur's death, my parents had begun taking children into their home to foster.

While fostering children was not uncommon at the time, there were several forces which motivated the fostering of children by Ma and Pa, one being a love of children. A foster daughter, Zoe, speaking from her experience in an account she wrote in July, 1994, of her foster mother (Measie[27] as she called her), stated that she "was a woman who loved children beside her very own children ..." In a subsequent letter to me, Zoe spoke of the "care and interest" her foster parents had for her and their "love and concern" for her, even though they did not know her consanguinal relatives. She expressed that she deeply appreciated these feelings and her care and love for them grew firm over the years and have lived on in her heart.

Henry drew attention to another motivating force in a tribute which he paid to our mother for a Mother's Day program held at Trinity Cathedral in Monrovia in 1978. He stated: ". . . always remembering her own good fortune, she tried to help and uplift as many of similar origins, as she could."

Ours was an extended family in the Liberian sense[28] and Ma had her hands full managing the home. Over time, 20 children plus my parents' first grandchild comprised the extended family.[29] The children taken into the family were mostly of indigenous background but also of settler background and of mixed background (settler and indigenous background). My parents' relationship and connections rather than ethnicity figured in the decisions regarding the children who became a part of the family. The composition of the home provided an interesting example of the crisscrossing of relations in the society and integration at work in it, we, their own children, of mixed background. This composition most likely did not go unnoticed in the society.

The linkages established between them and the consanguinal relatives of the children they fostered extended across wide areas of the country. Those of indigenous background sprang from six of the country's 16 major ethnic groups - Kru, Bassa, Vai, Gola, Kpelle and Gio. The earliest of the children taken in were: Elsie Frank, Peter Hall. William Grimes, Charlotte Madea Grimes (nickname Lottie).

Elsie was given to my parents for rearing as a teenager by her older sister, Mary Davis, whose husband, B. J. Davis, a leader in the Kru community in Monrovia and herself were close friends of Ma and Pa. Lottie was a toddler when she became a part of the family, unlike Elsie and most of the others, who joined the family as teenagers. She was brought to them by Pa's first cousin, Edwin Morgan, from his farm in Grand Bassa County.

By 1930, Ma and Pa had also taken Emmett Harmon, Lasanah Grimes and Edna Zoe Mayers (called Zoe). Emmett was the step-grandson of Sarah Harmon, younger sister of my mother's foster mother and son of her close friend, Annie Dennis Harmon and her husband, H. Lafayette Harmon. Zoe was a "mission girl" who had been sponsored by Nettie Mayers, an American missionary friend of Ma and Pa, who worked at Bromley Mission, where Zoe had been placed for fostering. She had spent brief periods visiting, with Miss Mayers - her Godmother and mine too - at our home. When Godma Mayers, who had left for the United States on furlough, changed her plans for continuing work in Liberia and did not return to Liberia, Ma and Pa brought Zoe into the family.

Later in the 1930s, Ma and Pa added Christine Morgan (nickname Chris), Garbea Grimes, Gladys Smith and Albert Kini Freeman (called Kini). Chris was the daughter of Edwin Morgan and his wife, Sarah, and was being entrusted to his cousin Louis and Victoria as her parents were separating. Gladys was brought from Lower Buchanan, Grand Bassa County, by Rose Brown, a friend of my mother and sister-in-law of Gladys' father, Edward Smith. She was about my age and would be my companion. Kini was Ma's nephew, son of Aunty Pai. He had studied at St. John Episcopal Mission[30] in Robertsport, Cape Mount, taken two years of teacher training courses there and taught in Episcopal schools in the Vai country. Subsequently, he had taken high school studies privately under Father Allen Bragg, an American missionary assigned to St. John and had come to Monrovia to continue his studies at Liberia College, entering the fourth year of the then Preparatory Department. By then, the first group, Lottie excepted, had married and established homes of their own.

Meeting the daily needs of my father, their own and the foster children kept my mother fully occupied. Seeing that everyone was properly fed and clothed; distributing the responsibilities of the household plus overseeing that they were carried out; and making appropriate arrangements for the education of the children were important tasks which claimed her attention. Sometimes, she had help from older people who resided in the home. One such person was a friend of the family, Miss Hester Johnson, who came to live with the family when she lost her home in a fire. My memories of "Donkey," as we affectionately called her go back to when I was approximately 10 years old. She was about 80 years old and a part of the extended family, mainly a "presence in the home. She took over the supervision of the home and us when both of our parents were out for periods in the day or on the rare occasions when they were both out of town.

Regarding the education of the children, Henry stated in the tribute referred to earlier, "Not fortunate to have access to the higher disciplines, she, nevertheless, had an awareness of the potential that could be released by a result of high intellectual pursuits. Thus, at home, she was the encouragement and the driving force in the education of her own and of her extended family. She accepted no excuse for poor grades."

One manifestation of her concern for the education of the children was her undertaking the home schooling of Marbue and me during the difficult period in the country of the early 1930s - he through grade one and I through grade three.

I have vivid recollections of this period - a definite time set aside each morning for us to be instructed by her. Nearby was a Catholic School, St. Patrick Elementary School. Its period bells, the sounds of children's voices in choral reading or reciting of the addition or multiplication tables and the voices of children at play during recess helped us feel it was "school time." It was a pleasant time and our progress was rapid, our mastery of the material setting the pace. For example, it took us about one-third of the time as it took students in the regular schools to do the pre-first studies - Primer I, Primer II and Infant Reader. The books used, the Royal Readers with their built-in phonetic approach to reading, were the same as they used. Ma was especially good in reading, penmanship, spelling and useful knowledge, a kind of vocabulary builder. She devoted considerable attention to teaching these subjects, less to arithmetic; perhaps either because it was not a favorite subject or one in which she was strong. Nevertheless, the overall foundations she laid were firm. We were able to hold our own when we began regular school.

Another example of the importance Ma attached to education was the extra effort she put forth over time to ensure that each child was enrolled in a school appropriate to the development of that child's capabilities. In charge of spending for the home and the children, she knew exactly what was needed.

One of the busiest times of the year for her was the beginning of the school year when she had to make sure that each child was ready for school - had the necessary clothes, books and school supplies and funds for paying tuition. She literally had to stretch Pa's earnings for each child to be covered. The main way she did this was by sewing much of the clothing that was needed - dresses, shirts, nightwear and girls' undergarments-thus reducing the outlay on clothing and freeing funds to be used for tuition and school supplies. Selecting good quality material at the most reasonable rates was her initial step in the performance of this task.

The other children and I took note of this effort, for we observed that a lot of the time she devoted to sewing was spent making household furnishings, such as curtains, cushions, pillow cases and mattress covers. She had her dresses made by seamstresses and often ripped and adjusted them to suit her taste, an idiosyncrasy, we thought. The excuse she gave for spending much time in altering clothes made for her was that she was hard to fit - not normally proportioned - short waist, small busts but large hips. Yet her overall size and shape seemed right. Although a little heavy, she always looked good. Thus, we often wondered and sometimes asked why she did not just outright make her dresses. Well, it seems that it took the challenge of preparing us for school to get her involved in making clothes, albeit clothes for us.

Another example of her belief in education's potential can be gleaned from the fact that she extended her efforts to ensure that people, other than her own children and those entrusted to the care of my father and herself, got a good education Fahnwullu's son, Feweh, provides an interesting illustration of this fact by a story of his own experience with her, which he wrote about while I was researching for this story.

In the late 1940s, some time after the death of his father, Feweh found himself short of funds to continue his schooling. He, therefore, decided to drop out of Liberia College where he was doing his collegiate studies and take a job with the Liberian Mining Company which, at the time, was just beginning its operations in Liberia. When his Cousin Jellemoh got this news, she sent for him and urged him to return to college, to persevere and complete his college education. She pointed out that the benefits of a college education far outweighed the benefits he could get from the immediate earnings that the job he had taken offered. The concrete means she offered to help him through the situation was to pay his tuition for two months and provide him what was, at that time, a very important meal - Sunday lunch. He would share it with her family. He heeded her, returned and studied until he received the Bachelor of Arts degree. Years later, he went on to graduate studies in the United States. In the 1960s, after he had received a Doctor of Philosophy degree and returned home, he was appointed by President Tubman to his Cabinet as Secretary of Education. He went to tell his Cousin Jellemoh the good news. Excited, she embraced him and said, "Feweh, you see? Suppose you had not listened to me and refused to go back to Liberia College, do you think you would be where you are today? You must thank God for what he has done for you and the Vai people."

The other major occurrence in the life of Ma and Pa was the change in Pa's career which took place during the early 1920s. For a period of 10 years, beginning around the time of their marriage, until 1922, he stuck with private law practice and became a successful and respected legal practitioner. Several times within this period, he refused to return to government service. Then, in 1922, during the Presidency of Charles Dunbar Burgess King, he accepted the appointment to the position of Attorney General, becoming a member of President King's Cabinet. From then on, his was service in the Government as a Cabinet official - Attorney General until 1932; Secretary of State, 1932-1933 - and from 1933 until his death in 1948, Chief Justice of the Supreme Court and Head of the Judicial Branch of Government. My mother was accordingly projected into the public eye as wife of an important Government official and remained so for the rest of my father's life. As was expected, she assumed added responsibilities as his helpmeet and became more visible in social and civic organizations.

At the time of my father's initial Cabinet appointment, my mother already belonged to the Culture Club of Monrovia, which had then recently been organized. This social group was composed of young women who set standards in etiquette and involved themselves in community projects, such as improving and beautifying historic sites in Monrovia at a time when the Municipality had not taken on this responsibility. The Club played an important role in the life of the community.[31]

For one thing, attention to the proper ways of behaving and doing things was still front and center. A person's general demeanor, social graces, style of dress and appearance, as well as the décor of a person's home figured strongly in how that person was regarded in the society. The pace was quite naturally set by the élite. Thus, a man of some prominence, whose wife was from a coastal county, made sure once they moved to Monrovia that his wife formed a relationship as quickly as possible with women who were part of the Monrovia élite society. This ensured her adjustment to Monrovia and acceptance in Monrovia élite society. Some of the women of the Culture Club served as "big sisters" to such women. Illustrative of this is the story told of E.C.B. Jones who, when he and his young wife, Georgia, first moved to Monrovia, took her and introduced her to my mother and Mrs. M. Eva McGill Hilton, and of Isaac Whisnant, who did the same for his wife, Louise (nickname Lu) when he brought her from Cape Palmas to Monrovia.

Reverting to the projects undertaken by the Club, a notable one was the fencing in of the Government Square, where the historic Hall of Representatives Building, which housed the Legislature and the Supreme Court, was located and the landscaping of its grounds. The Government Square thus became a center of attraction, a place where people went to enjoy fresh air and relax and, in later years, also listen to the music played by the Liberian Frontier Force Band, under the direction of its talented Bandmaster, Chrislow. Music by this Band became a late Sunday afternoon feature for several years.

The Government Square Project, financed by fund-raising activities of the Club, must have struck a sentimental chord in my mother, for the Ashmun Street side of the Square was opposite the building that was initially the Executive Mansion.[32] That building, situated on Ashmun Street almost at its junction with Buchanan Street, was where she lived, with her foster parents, President and Mrs. Cheeseman, when she first was taken to Monrovia as a child, seven years old.

Another example of my mother's efforts in community service was the leadership role she assumed in new organizations, the Liberian Girls Guide, for example. This counterpart to the Boys Scouts was founded in the 1920s by Mrs. Adeline King, wife of President King. My mother was one of its original Council members.

During the 1930s and 1940s, as the role of the central Government expanded, importance was increasingly being attached to holding positions in Government. Despite this fact and the social standing of my parents, they kept the common touch. There was a flow of people to their home - friend, neighbors, acquaintances and strangers. Whether or not their friends and neighbors had made upward strides like them, they were welcome to their home. Together they reminisced of old times, shared a good laugh and enjoyed the company of one another. In my time, one of the examples which riveted itself on my mind was the relationship Ma maintained with a girlhood friend of hers who had fallen into hard times and poverty and was generally looked down on. Good times with her she continued to have. I remember the fun, laughter and joy which filled our home whenever she visited. Their feelings for each other were clearly mutual. It seemed nothing had changed since they were growing up in Edina in the homes of two prominent families.

Such regard for people made an indelible impression on all of us who came directly under my parents' influence ; we, their own children and the children entrusted to their care. In fact, my parents' love and respect for people endeared them to people in their community and throughout the country, helped to give meaning and purpose to their lives and opened doors for us.

An interesting example of the challenging role my father's position placed my mother in relates to the extra responsibility she had to assume during the period 1931-1933 when he had to make a number of trips to Geneva and remain there for a considerable period each time, defending Liberia's cause before the League of Nations. Liberia had been charged with the practices of slavery and forced labor and placed on the Mandate agenda of the League. At the time the crisis began, Antoine Sottile, a foreign national, was Liberia's Envoy Extraordinary and Minister Plenipotentiary, Permanent Delegate to the League of Nations and the International Labour Organization. In 1931, shortly after Edwin James Barclay succeeded King as President, filling King's unexpired term, he appointed my father Associate Delegate to the League to assist Minister Sottile. Barclay felt that it was important to have a Liberian at the League. He knew that my father, then Attorney General, would be an asset in the negotiations. In 1932, when President in his own right, Barclay named him Secretary of State, giving him the authority to act in the country's behalf whenever he attended the various meetings of the Council of the League and the Committee the Council established in connection with the crisis. Alone for long stretches of time at intervals during these years, Ma had to keep the home going and to supervise us, three in 1931 under nine; Henry, a teenager; and the foster children, mainly teenagers. It was much work but a worthwhile experience and having such demands on her time helped her to focus on other than the anxieties my father's travel and his absence from home caused.

At the time, travel from Liberia to Europe was by the English, Dutch and German mail boats which plied the West African coast on a regular but rather infrequent basis, especially when it came to making stops at Monrovia. There was no harbor and so the ships anchored out in the deep and were serviced from the shore by surf boats. This scene was all too familiar to my mother from her girlhood days in Edina and she knew the dangers and risks. Sometimes, my father had to catch the ships in difficult weather and at awkward times of the day or night. It all depended on whether a ship was making a regular call at the Port of Monrovia or stopping by special arrangement, dropping anchor just long enough for him to board. There was also the sharp difference in weather that had to be endured in case travel had to be made to Geneva during the winter months, which happened to be the dry season and hottest time in Liberia. Finally, the stress from the hassling negotiations, the problems of travel and the slim budget provided for the trips, given the poor financial situation the country was experiencing, took a toll on my father's health as the months went by. My mother was concerned, especially during the latter months of this period, as to how he would fare from one trip to the next.

Quite naturally, my father's return from each trip brought joy to my mother and us. Just having him back home with the family meant a lot. Everyone could enjoy his company and play games with him and he could share some of the responsibilities my mother had to shoulder during his absence. Occasionally, there were goodies for the family. A memorable example was the occasion when he brought back bicycles - one for Rudolph and one for me - and a toy car for Marbue that he could drive himself around in. Rarities in Liberia at the time, they were enjoyed not only by us but also by the children of our neighborhood and our other friends.

For my mother, there was also the opportunity of hearing the high points of the Geneva trip and of accomplishments my father had been able to make. Whether it was getting Liberia transferred from the Mandate agenda of the League of Nations to the regular agenda; getting the ear and support of delegates from countries like Poland, Spain and Italy to balance the weight of the powers such as Britain and France which had colonies in Africa adjoining Liberia and interest in Liberia's territory; or putting forth reservations to the League Plan of Assistance, she could share with him the history that was being made. She encouraged and cheered him until he was able to win Liberia's case at the League. Those international powers which had made a bid to have Liberia mandated were frustrated in their efforts. Liberia remained a free and sovereign state. A successful mission indeed! There was celebration at our home and throughout the nation.

With this battle behind, my mother had my father at home to face with her and the larger family the sadness of the final days in the life of his mother. She had already begun ailing during the latter period of his travels to Geneva and had been moved from the home she shared with Aunt Mal to the home of Aunty Mai and Uncle Richard. It was now more than 20 years since my parents' marriage and Ma had enjoyed a mutually loving and warm relationship with her mother-in-law. Now, she was ill and needed attention and care. Ma stood with Aunty Mai to do all they could for her. It was a sad time, knowing that she would not recover, but Ma was thankful to God she could be by her side, thankful too that she had contributed her share of the grandchildren she had enjoyed. With Aunty Mai and other members of the family, she stood right to the end, sharing the vigil over her during the final hours of her life which ended early in the night on May 11, 1934.

Again, my parents experienced the pain of the loss of a close one which it took them time to adjust to. Also, with only two of the 11 siblings of my father's mother left, his Aunt Mal and Uncle Arthur, the realization began to settle in that the family torch would soon be handed to his generation. These deaths came a few years later - Aunt Mal in 1936 at the age of 95 and Uncle Arthur in 1938, at the age of 84. There was, of course, sadness for the family with each of these deaths but also thankfulness to God for their long lives and the blessings their longevity had bestowed upon the family.

Meanwhile, meeting the challenges posed by the day-to-day management of the home continued to claim a considerable portion of Ma's time. Modern amenities, such as electricity, running water and telephones were non-existent at the time in Liberia, Monrovia not excepted. Thus, such household tasks as preserving food, cooking meals, getting the household clothes washed and ironed, getting water for bathing, cooking and washing were slow and tedious. And, yes, given her meticulousness, there were the many tasks involved in keeping a three-story frame house spic and span, door knobs shining, and the floors, woodwork and furniture clean and free of termites and other insects which could easily infest wood and destroy floors, interior fittings and furniture. Fortunately, the problem of getting water was easier than a number of homes in Monrovia faced, as there was a well in the yard which supplied water year round, serving our family and some of our neighbors as well. It seldom went dry during the dry season and then, only for very short periods.

Ma was an early riser. She awakened at 5:00 a.m. and aroused the household to begin the day. There usually was some paid household help, but for the most part, she distributed the tasks among the children. Saturday was a particularly demanding day. It was the day for general household cleaning up, changing of beddings and linens and getting these out for washing. Also, until well into the 1940s, before there was electricity in Monrovia which simplified the preservation of food, it was an important day for buying, processing and preserving food for the week. This was especially true for beef, as cows were slaughtered on Saturdays and beef, entrails and cow's tail purchased then. In my time, the day began earlier than normal so that my father and one of my brothers, who accompanied him, could get to the market early enough to get the desired quantity of meat, the right cuts and meat that was fresh. Then came preparation of the meals for Saturday; baking meat for Sunday lunch, the main meal of the day; and preserving meat for the rest of the week by parboiling, salting and other means. Although much was going on, our assignments on three different floors, Ma kept a check on each of us to ensure that each person's assigned responsibility was carried out. I often wondered and marveled at her ability to do so.

Lightening the workload was a major challenge for her and she found interesting ways to achieve this. I recall how she reduced the time and effort spent on the actual washing of white clothes by having us boil them on the stove for about ten minutes in a five gallon container before they were washed. Amazing how much dirt was removed and how little effort had to be exerted in washing after this process!

Ma often had a paid cook, but she devoted a lot of time and attention to the preparation of food. It is interesting to note that she almost always had to teach the cook. In those days, cooks usually learned on the job.

In the traditional Liberian societies where the sexual division of labor was clear and distinct, cooking was women's work. While not exactly true in Liberian "sophisticated society," there was striking similarity, as women did much of the cooking. Many women felt that the way to a man's heart was through his stomach. Many wives believed that good cooking was an important way to keep their husbands. Women accepted the home as their place and cooking a central part of the work of the home.

Ma took pride in being a good cook and relished seeing her husband enjoy his meals. In fact, she literally pampered him when it came to his meals. Even his drink - tea, cocoa and occasionally bovril - was made for him by her or one of us whom she had taught. Mealtime was special and the atmosphere had to be pleasant. Once anyone introduced into the conversation something unpleasant,

Pa simply reminded, "I am eating." Everyone understood that the unpleasant note had to be dropped and something pleasant introduced instead.

Sometimes, after enjoying the basic meal, midday or evening, Pa would jokingly ask, "Victoria, where is the aukum?" She knew this meant time for dessert and she would serve some one of the favorite pastries she was good at making, for example, cake, pawpaw (papaya) or pumpkin pie, bread pudding, potato custard, to name some. Or it might be something as simple as blanc mange or agidi, a corn preparation that was made and sold locally, mashed to the proper consistency by adding water and milk and sweetening with sugar.

Making preserves and jellies was one of the occasional tasks Ma engaged in. The favorites were pineapple preserve, guava preserve and stewed mangoes. The exercise took a lot of time, but she delighted in it and often involved us. It provided a means of utilizing pineapples in particular but also other fruits grown on the small farm she and Pa had about 40 miles from our home and making something tasty for the table while cutting cost on the purchase of jams and jellies. Also utilized was the cocoa which was grown there and processed into small balls which made a delicious drink. How rich and tasty this drink was! I remember preferring it to the cocoa and similar drinks sold in the stores, which had been processed abroad through industrial means and bereft of the richness the cocoa beans had when hand processed locally.

Sometimes, Ma used her cooking skills in public service. In her day, there were no professional caterers in Liberia. Food for official functions, such as the annual Independence Day receptions which were held, especially in Monrovia and other functions given by the President was prepared by women who donated their services. Women whose husbands were in the Cabinet and other high governmental positions were normally called upon. So were women from different walks of life who were known for their skills in cooking and baking. The President's wife would form a team of women for each such occasion. I remember Ma being called upon from time to time during the 1930s and 1940s. She enjoyed contributing her share to the services required. During these times, the women prided themselves in their varying skills in cooking, making pastries and baking, which they were putting to use and shared many pleasant moments while performing these tasks, socializing across class and ethnic lines.

We were always central, however and a major concern. Attendance at school, work in the home and recreation were essential aspects of the day for each child. So were the daily prayers which began each day. Recreation time was late afternoon when the rays of the sun had begun to lose their intensity. A main playground was the section of Broad Street, right in front of our house, which simplified for my mother supervision of us at play. Of course, the street at this end of the city had not then been fixed and opened to traffic. It was a veritable playground. There we and the children of the neighborhood often gathered to play different games. A very popular game was football (soccer), usually played by the boys but sometimes joined in by the girls. I recall the happy times we had on that field.

Discipline was a learning process and the goal self-discipline. Zoe notes the importance given to family gatherings, prayers for example and the fact that each child was expected to be present at them. If absent, she points out, a child had to have a good excuse or be punished, one way children learned to be where they were supposed to be.

The child rearing process brought much satisfaction and many moments of happiness. But it also had its moments of disappointment. Regarding the latter, I recall the problem when it came to dressing me, for early I showed a taste in dress that was plain and unlike my mother's fancy taste. I simply did not enjoy being dressed up with the bows, ruffles and other fancy clothes of little girls. Party time and other dress-up occasions for me could be annoying for her. She was less inclined to indulge this plain taste of mine in dress than my preference for the games my brothers enjoyed, like playing ball and riding hoops as opposed to playing with dolls, which I seldom did. It would be years hence for her to accept this taste of mine. And interestingly, when, with the dawn of the nativistic movement in Liberia during the late 1960s, I adopted and increasingly went for a nativistic style of dress, using the lappa and buba, she always admired my clothes and complimented me. Not that my plain taste in dress had gone away, but she had grown to appreciate it. Moreover, she looked beyond it and was pleased I could accentuate my African identity through dress, something the times had not allowed her and educated women of her generation to do.

Before my 10th year, a high point for the family was the graduation of Henry from Liberia College in November, 1935, with the Bachelor of Arts degree. For some time, he had exhibited a technological bent, but there was no institution in Liberia at the time that offered such training. Our parents encouraged him to take advantage of the educational opportunities that were available. Accordingly, he studied at Liberia College and completed its liberal arts program. Simultaneously, he explored opportunities for technological exposure, beginning by working as an apprentice to Monsieur Biondi, a French national, who was in charge of the then newly established Liberian Government Radio Station. He gained considerable practical experience in radio communication and learned a lot in the process, becoming a pioneer in the Liberian Government Radio and Telecommunications Service. In later years, he pursued formal studies in this specialty, first, for a few months in Dakar, Senegal and then for several years at the Radio Corporation of America (RCA) Institute in New York, United States, from which he received a diploma in 1941.

Henry had reached his majority and was off to a successful career, but Ma still had the younger children to take care of and supervise. At the time of Henry's graduation from college, Rudolph, then 12, had successfully completed grade seven, his first year in junior high school at the College of West Africa (CWA), a high school which, at that time, included the upper elementary grades (fourth, fifth and sixth).[33] I, then nine, had ended my first year in a regular school - CWA - successfully completing grade four. Marbue, age seven, had completed grade two in a private elementary school.

Of the children being fostered, Emmett Harmon left Liberia in 1932 for studies at Howard University in Washington, D.C., United States, from which he returned in 1934. Lottie completed her studies at the E. V. Day Girls' School, a Lutheran Mission boarding school for girls situated on the St. Paul River at Harrisburg. Years later, she would begin and complete high school and studies in professional nursing and go on to long and dedicated service to the country as a surgical nurse. Kini entered the Freshman Class of Liberia College and readily excelled. He had an enviable background in Latin, the classical language being required and taught at Liberia College at that time and was sought by his class-mates and other schoolmates for assistance with their Latin assignments. Zoe was then teaching at Bethany, having been transferred from Bromley Mission where she had completed her studies and begun teaching.

At the time, only the academic subjects were taught in the formal school system. Music, art and subjects which provided saleable vocational skills, such as typewriting and shorthand, were not. To study the two last named subjects, a child had to do so in one of the private classes offered instruction in the afternoon. One such class was that of Mrs. Eugenia Simpson Cooper, begun in 1934, the first offering Gregg shorthand plus typewriting. Our parents saw many advantages in training of this type and enrolled Rudolph when he was a sixth grader in Mrs. Cooper's private class. Rudolph recalls Mrs. Cooper's reluctance to accept him in the class then, as she felt he was too young. But Ma was confident he could succeed and convinced Mrs. Cooper to give him a try. Rudolph also recalls his own initial disinterest and playful attitude toward these studies. However, on Ma's urging, he showed a remarkable capability after his first few months of study. I was enrolled several years later. By then, Rudolph already had begun to use his skills in Gregg shorthand and typewriting in office work with Dr. Rudolph Fuszek, the government medical officer then responsible for Liberia's public health service. Ma especially was anxious for us to learn shorthand and typewrit-ing. Her anxiety grew both out of the fact that these subjects had practical value and because she considered our studying them compensation for educational opportunities she had missed. Such studies were not available in the country in her time.

The other area in which Ma and Pa wanted us, the younger children, to acquire proficiency was music. During the early 1940s, they enrolled us in pri-vate music classes begun around that time by Miss Alice Roberts who had immi-grated to Liberia from the United States about a decade earlier and had by then moved from Greenville, Sinoe County and settled in Monrovia. Ma saw that our time was appropriately divided for study of the subjects we were taking in school, music practice, responsibilities in the home and recreation. One outcome of the music classes was that the home became more and more lively with music as each of us practiced and played at our respective level. There were piano solos and piano duets, Marbue and I often playing the duets.

It was not long, however, before it was clear that Marbue had a special talent and needed to devote more time to music to cultivate his talent. He excelled

Rudolph and me. Gifted, he soon played by notes and by ear all types of music (hymns, classical music and popular music). He practically lived at the piano, practicing his music lessons and playing tunes he loved. Sometimes, Ma had to make him get up from the piano to take care of his responsibilities in the home. Of course, she struck a delicate balance, allowing him ample time to play the piano. She and Pa enjoyed listening to him and seeing his music become a drawing card, bringing many of his friends to the home to gather around the piano to hear him play and enjoy the music. They encouraged this activity. His crowning moment was at the musical recital given by the students of Miss Alice Roberts at the Cox Memorial Auditorium in March, 1943. Then 14 years old, Marbue played Beethoven's Moonlight Sonata, charming and astounding his audience. No one dreamed that it was his finalé.

Meanwhile, World War II was continuing to rage. Henry had returned from the United States where he had successfully pursued studies in radio technology at RCA Institute. The family had grown to include another of Aunty Pai's sons, George Molondoi Freeman, younger brother of Kini. George had completed his high school studies at St. John's, Robertsport and had come to Monrovia to enter Liberia College and begin collegiate studies. Later in the 1940s, there were the following additions to the family: Jackson Fiah Doe, Momo Freeman and Mary Zina Freeman (called Zina). Jackson was the son of Clan Chief Sawah Doe of the Gblolay Clan, Sanniquellie, then Central Province, later Nimba County and his wife, Kwarwoh Doe. He was one of several sons sent by his father at that time to become part of the family of various Government officials. His joining the family is an example of one way alliances were forged in Liberia between indigenous élite and settler élite, first by coastal ethnic groups and later, interior ethnic groups, such as the Gios, from which Jackson sprang. Momo was Aunty Pai's youngest son and Zina her youngest daughter and the first of her girls to be allowed to study in the Western-oriented educational system. Although they were younger and began their studies from our home at a much lower academic level than their brothers, neither remained as long as their brothers. Momo was the child designated by his parents, both of whom were strong believers in the Islamic faith, to go the route of Islam, so his stay was the shortest. He was withdrawn to pursue studies in the Koran and Islam. No persuasion of my parents could change this course for him.

There were favorable and unfavorable aspects to the war. Beginning with the favorable, Liberia was strategically located and very much needed by the Allied powers to facilitate their movement of people, weapons, equipment and materials for launching and successfully carrying out their North African campaign, with the goal of liberating Europe from the Germans. The Government of Liberia allowed the United States to establish two bases for this purpose - Bensonfield near Robertsport, Cape Mount and Robertsfield (now Roberts International Airport) near Harbel. Thus, air flights were made possible between the United States and the African continent by the shortest and most direct route. In addition, Liberia became a supplier of natural rubber, vital to the war effort, when the normal suppliers, the Far East countries, could no longer supply this important product. Interesting it was to see how the world powers that had been in a hostile and confrontational stance regarding Liberia during the nation's crisis with the League of Nations during the 1930s now changed their relationship to one of friendship and cooperation. Liberia declared war on the side of the Allies in late January, 1944.

One clear result of Liberia's strategic role in this war, even before the country's formal declaration of war, was the improved economic situation which resulted from two main sources: (1) Funds generated directly and indirectly from the bases established by the United States at Bensonfield and Robertsfield and, (2) Increased production of rubber, accompanied by a soaring in the price of rubber per pound.

The economic boost, however, was not without its problems. For example, more money found its way into the economy and as this occurred; an increasing emphasis was placed on material things. Even worse for the moral situation was the fact that the soldiers stationed at the bases increasingly became a part of the life of Monrovia. When they had brief leaves from the bases, they often headed to Monrovia where some of them spent much time partying, drinking and carousing and promoting prostitution. As this change in Monrovia became more and more apparent, my parents, like many other parents, found it posed a real challenge to the rearing of children. They had to ensure that their home remained a moral bastion, for the city began losing the quietness and the societal standards they had known.

A challenge of another dimension was the acute shortage of food. Government resorted to the rationing of food, especially rice, the staple food of the country and other basic food commodities such as sugar and flour. In fact, the war exacerbated a situation regarding the adequacy of the supply of locally produced food that the increase in the population of Monrovia had created.[34] Ma, like other housewives, had the tasks of making the food supplies, which were rationed, last between the designated times for rationing and also of finding ways of incorporating into the household diet new foods which were given out as part of the rations. One such food was hominy grits, given as a substitute for rice, a family typically receiving 50 percent of its allotment for rice in rice and the other 50 percent in hominy grits, commonly referred to at the time as "cargo." Ma also had to use more locally produced food and contribute to the increased production of such food through her home garden and small farm.

The end of the War in 1945 with victory for the Allies was a time of rejoicing and celebration in Liberia, as in other allied countries. Unprecedented change was on the horizon for the country as a result of the war, but this was not visualized. People were caught in the joy victory brings after a long period of violent conflict, with its resulting deaths and destruction.

There were other happy times in the 1940s, these of a personal nature. They centered around our accomplishments, as the story will reveal later. There were also the periods of sadness, occasioned by the deaths of two loved ones - Ma's "baby," Marbue and her beloved husband.

Marbue's death occurred on Decoration Day, March 10, 1943, two days after the musical recital at which he played so well. It was a shock not only to our parents and the family, but the entire community. Young though he was, he was well known and loved in the community. There was an outpouring of affection and sympathy for our family.

As to the circumstances surrounding the death, Marbue, Rudolph and George had gone with a group on a holiday excursion, traveling by motor boat from Monrovia to the Lutheran Mission in Harrisburg. Such opportunities were rare and Marbue, like others who went on the trip, looked forward to happy times. All was going well. Marbue was at the piano entertaining a group when a few friends invited him to go swimming in the St. Paul River. That was nothing strange, for in those days when the country lacked swimming pools, people swam in the rivers and the ocean for pleasure. However, the area was more treacherous than he and the others who had gone for a swim knew. They were hardly in the water when Marbue went down and did not return to the surface. It was felt that he hit his head on a rock and drowned. After a considerable search, the body was recovered from the river by Miss Norma Bloomquist, an American missionary who worked for the Lutheran Mission at Harrisburg, an act for which the family has remained eternally grateful. What a blow for our parents, us siblings and the rest of the family, especially Rudolph and George who were on the trip, although not at the site of the drowning!

On the day of the excursion, Ma was not at home. She was about 40 miles from Monrovia on the farm near Kakata where she had gone to get a few things done. When Henry and Stanley, who Pa had sent for her, reached her, they tried to break the bad news slowly by telling her first that Marbue had fallen ill. However, a night or two earlier she had had a premonition, so she questioned, "sick, not dead"? The dream she had had was identical to that which she experienced just before Arthur's death. The only difference was that this time she saw her foster mother leading Marbue away. Well, the three of them made the car trip to Monrovia without Henry and Stanley telling her exactly what had happened. However, by the time they neared our home, she saw that a crowd had gathered in and outside the home. Her worse fears were confirmed. Marbue was indeed dead!

This death Ma seemed not to be able to get over. She spent months weeping and wailing over this loss. In fact, it was not until almost a year after when she and Pa took into the home their first grandchild, Henry and Gladys' son, James Rudolph (nickname Jim), then about one year old, that she began to get over this grief. He helped to wipe away her tears like she as a little child had done for her foster mother more than 50 years earlier.

How did our parents cope with this sudden death and loss, the sadness, grief and pain that it brought? Amidst their deep grief, their Christian beliefs were evident and this fact spoke volumes.

In Monrovia, at that time, as in the rest of the country, people invariably attributed to witchcraft the death of a promising person, especially when that death was due to an illness that was not understood or was sudden. There were those who wanted to do just this and blame Marbue's death on his friends, whom they claimed were jealous of him. Our parents would have none of this. They had been sufficiently involved in the life of Marbue and his friends to know that there was mutual love between them. More importantly, they saw God in the situation and knew that His ways are past man's understanding. They were aware that God reckons time quite differently to how it is measured in the eyes of human beings. Besides, earth is not our home. One of the hymns Pa chose for the funeral, "Brief Life Is Here Our Portion," words by St. Bernard of Cluny, partly expressed their thoughts. The song speaks of sorrow being brief here and care short-lived, contrasting this with the life "there" that "knows no ending" and is "tearless." The concluding lines of the first verse are: O happy retribution, Short toil, eternal rest, for mortals and for sinners A mansion with the blest!

In the last verse, there is reference to an awakening morning when "shadows flee away" and "each true-hearted servant" shines as the day. The verse concludes: For God our King and Portion, in fullness of his grace. We then shall see for ever, And worship face to face.

Our parents had not only themselves to think of. They also had to help us cope with the family's big loss. First, there was the psychological impact the death had on Rudolph who was in Harrisburg although not on the river bank either at the time the group went to swim or the time of the drowning. He took the death hard, suffering palpitations of the heart. He was so grief stricken and worried he behaved as though he was losing his mind. To soothe his pain, he was sent to spend some time with Uncle Richard and Aunty Mai who had three sons about his age - Reid , Richard and Louis. Everything else was done to help him get over the shock, including moving him from the room he had shared with Marbue and George to a different one in the house. As for me who was nearest Marbue in age, my main companion was gone. It was a very sad time for me. I did not even want to touch the piano. Indeed, there was sadness for all of the children. Moreover, we had to come to grips with the reality of death. None of us knows at whose door death will knock and when.

It helped the family to discuss some of what had happened as the three boys contemplated going on the excursion. For example, Pa was known by all of the children never to change a no answer given to a request from any of us. Interestingly, he made a change when it came to the excursion. His initial response to the boys' request to go was no. Then, he remembered that within recent times, Rudolph and Marbue had been negligent in attending the daily morning family prayers. He decided that a yes could be given for the trip if they satisfactorily expressed in writing their feelings about this neglect and their intention for the future with respect to this important matter. Rudolph wrote a short letter, expressing regret for his past action and promising to do better in the future. Marbue wrote also - a rather long letter. He conveyed the same feelings in a letter so moving and touching, that Pa changed his original no to yes - on the strength of that letter.

There was, however, one condition - the boat by which they were traveling would have to be safe for the trip. Pa was anxious regarding the safety of the boat, an anxiety due to the fact that at that time, it was not uncommon to overload the riverboats as well as the trucks and other means of land transportation, which often resulted in accidents. So, he sent Henry to make the check and give the yes for the trip if the boat was safe. Well, the boat was not overloaded and everything was in order. The possibility of an accident occurring while on the trip was not thought about. Yet, that was the reality to be faced at the end of the day.

Another member of the family was gone. There was physical separation from Arthur and now Marbue. But they lived on as a pleasant part of the family's memory and the family knew it had been blessed by their lives. Yes, we gave thanks to God for having given each of them to the family for the respective period of time each had lived.

Life is indeed checkered. This fact was clearly illustrated in the 1940s in the life of the family. There were joyous occasions ushering in the decade, then this sad experience of Marbue's death, followed by more occasions of joy and happiness. Success was crowning in various ways the efforts of the foster children, Rudolph and me and foundations were being laid for distinctive contributions to the country in the future by us.

The first of the joyous occasions preceding Marbue's death and ushering in the 1940s was Rudolph's graduation from CWA as dux of his class in November, 1940. In March of the following year, he entered Liberia College. Just before his graduation from high school was the marriage of Zoe to Momolu Freeman, then a clerk in the office of the Superintendent of Cape Mount County. The wedding took place on Dec. 26, 1940, at St. John Irving Memorial Church, the Episcopal Church in Robertsport, the Rev. J.D.K. Baker, the officiant. Zoe went on to build her family there, having four children, all girls, and to continue her work in teaching at Bethany. The fourth significant and happy event in this period was Kini's graduation from Liberia College as dux of his class of five, all male, in November, 1942. After graduation, he went on to teach in the preparatory (high school) division of Liberia College and some years later, after studies in the United States, head the Division of Fisheries in the then Department of Agriculture and Commerce. The other important step he took following his graduation from college was a traditional marriage to the young Vai maiden, Zina Sambollah. After years of work with Government, he turned his attention to and became a pivotal figure in the development of the village of Mani, Gawula, Cape Mount, the welfare of the people of the village central to development.

The happy events which followed Marbue's death were my graduation from CWA as dux of my class in November, 1943, and my entry into Liberia College in early 1944 at a time when only a handful of girls in the country were continuing their education beyond high school. At the end of the same year, Rudolph graduated from Liberia College as dux of his class of four, all male. Another celebration was the marriage of Chris on Aug. 4, 1945, to James Dossen Richards, a 1938 graduate of Liberia College. At that time, she had gone to live with her father who had remarried and had acquired a home of his own in Monrovia where he lived when the Liberian Senate, of which he was then a member, was in session. The other two important academic events were the graduation from Liberia College of George in 1946 and of me in 1947 as dux of my class of seven - five male and two female. These graduations brought to six, Pa included, the number in our immediate family who to that date had completed the nation's highest institution of learning. Success was crowning the efforts of the natural born children and the children in the extended family.

At the time of my graduation, Rudolph had made the big accomplishment of getting admitted to Harvard Law School. He had left for Cambridge, Massachusetts, United States, to study law there, entering the last class of Harvard's accelerated program in Law, which was established at the end of World War II to facilitate the study of US veterans at Harvard Law School. Almost a year later, I left for Cambridge to study for a Master's degree at Radcliffe College.

Naturally, our parents were pleased at the progress and success each of the children of the family had made. However, when it came to me, it was like the fulfillment of a dream for me to have the best possible opportunity for study and for them to be able to finance my study venture abroad. This was so not merely because I was the only girl of their own children but also because I had exhibited a high potential and their hopes for me were high. Also, they did not share the generally restrictive view in the Liberia of that day of what girls could or should achieve academically. Besides, there was still no opportunity in the country for graduate studies. There was added joy for I, then almost 22 years old, had fallen in love and received a proposal for marriage from the charming and promising Kedrick Wellington Brown. Moreover, Kedrick had been persuaded to let the marriage take place after my return from one year of graduate studies in the United States.

In now more than 35 years of marriage, Ma and Pa had together watched their own children and most of the children they were fostering reach maturity. The exceptions were their little grandson, Jim, then six years old and starting off to school and Jackson Doe, then 14 years old, attending CWA in the junior high school and excelling in his studies, a forerunner to the remarkable educational achievement he would make and distinguished service he would render the country in education and in political life.[35]   We children, for the most part, had made satisfactory progress in our studies, the older ones toward their career goals as well.

Our home had been a source of joy and strength for our parents and the family. It had broadened experiences and provided insights for all of the children, across settler and indigenous lines and opened the way to challenging opportunities for us.

CHAPTER 7

Example and Precepts - Vic's Guiding Words[36]

My mother's life was an articulation of her philosophy, for she believed example was better than precepts and actions spoke louder than words. Through her own life; her influence on my father; their own children; and the children who became a part of their family, what she believed and stood for was manifest.

She and my father were grounded in Christian principles and shared similar values. However, their manner of instruction in the home and communication of beliefs was different. Hers was, for the most part, simple and informal. At home with the children, while he spent many hours away each day at work, she had numerous situations in day-to-day living to deal with us. As these situations presented opportunities while she went about her daily tasks, she often used witty expressions to highlight what she believed and considered important guidelines to living. Some of these expressions were inspired by the Bible, others by her physical environment and some by her life experiences and their context. For example, when we children would build air castles, as we did at times, she would sometimes say: "Mr. Talk is all right but Mr. Do is the man."

This was a reminder that things are easier said than done; also that how a person behaves and what actions that person takes provide a better idea of what that person stands for than what that person says.

The expression made a strong impression on me. I recall, for example, how these words dominated my thoughts at one of the most demanding periods of my life -- when I became President of the University of Liberia and faced the challenges of that position. I always felt as though I needed to talk as little as possible and demonstrate by action the bold steps that had to be taken. I tried to popularize the expression, "Mr. Talk is all right but Mr. Do is the man."

Not merely by using it on significant occasions, from the eve of my ascendancy to the position in late March, 1978, but translating it into action, up to August, 1984 when my Presidency ended. I kept clear goals in mind and worked to build a Team of University Faculty and Staff at varying levels. As a Team, our work won national and international acclaim and reflected the vision, dreams and high hopes which I had for the institution and which the Team shared.

The undergirding force in Ma's life was her belief in God. Her Christian exposure came early and she believed God was the Almighty, Ruler of the universe, all-wise, merciful and good. A favorite expression of hers indicative of this belief was the first line of the hymn, "Whate'r my God ordains is right. . ."

Hers was a personal relationship with God. She often prayed as though she was talking to a close friend and her faith was unshakeable. She believed God's promises were sure and she stood on them and encouraged those close to her to do the same. A classic example was when she was consoling me, then 35 years old, deep in grief and mourning the sudden loss of my dear husband, Kedrick. She reminded me that God is "Father of the fatherless and defendeth the cause of the widows. . ." (Psalm 69:5) and she added, "Hold God to His promises."

I had been fatherless for years and had just become a widow also. She knew God would take care of me and wanted me to lean on Him in this assurance.

There would be increased responsibilities on me, resulting from my having become a single parent, relative our family of five - our own three small children, 10 years old and under and the slightly older two children, relatives of mine whom we were fostering. However, I did not need to worry, for "God fits the back for the burden."

Naturally, prayers were central to her life and daily prayers early in the morning were an important part of the life of the family. Everyone in the home was expected to be present. There the family gave thanks to God for the new day and drew strength to face it. The daily routine for family prayers consisted of reading of the Scriptures and prayers led by Pa or herself. This was expanded on Sundays to include singing of a hymn, explanation of the lessons for the day, as set forth in the Episcopal Book of Common Prayer for the particular Sunday in the Church's year, and a recital of the collect for the Sunday from memory by each child. On Sundays, there was also regular attendance at Church in the morning by the entire family and Sunday School in the afternoon by the children.

Christian principles embodied in the Ten Commandments and the Golden Rule were guides to living. We had to learn them not merely for the sake of knowing them but also to apply them in day-to-day living. To love one's neighbor as oneself is not an easy standard to attain. However, each of us was to strive toward this standard which was to be reflected in our relations with people. In this connection, we had to learn to be sensitive to the feelings of others. For example, each of us had to learn to recognize and acknowledge a wrong which he/she had committed and apologize to the person affected. Sometimes one of us would say, "I forgive, but I won't forget." Well, that was not the type of apology allowed. A child wronged was expected to forgive, once an apology was offered and to forget.

Ma knew that she had been blessed by God in many ways. The circumstances of her life were testimonial to that and she always wanted to share God's blessings with others. One way was to help bring sunshine into the lives of others by helping them appreciate the goodness of God. Thus, she always radiated a happy disposition that came from the inner joy she always seemed to have. She greeted people warmly and made them feel special. For those in need who visited, she shared to help them meet their basic needs, one of them being food. One person who visited her home on a number of occasions and needed such help remarked that she was always generous with food. Her home was home not only for her own children but also for other children entrusted to the care of her and her husband and relatives who suffered deep disappointment and were on the verge of despair. Among this latter group was one of the nieces of her foster mother, Anna, who had to end what turned out to be an abusive marital relationship. Encouraging her to be a part of their home as long as necessary, she and Pa provided her the comfort and strength she needed to regain confidence in herself, readjust to life and reestablish herself in a home of her own.

Consideration for others and sharing were two other important values for Ma. An expression that she sometimes used to sensitize us to these values was: "Don't take the last pea out of the pod."

By this, in certain situations, she meant that when there was anything to be divided, none of us should take more than his/her fair share. Taking the "last pea" --the last food item out of a dish, for example, could mean that someone would go without or have less than a fair share. The expression was, however, like a code and was sometimes used in a different context and had another meaning. If, for example, we were on our way out of the home to a party or other gathering, whether informal at the home of someone or a public function, she might say, "Don't take the last pea out of the pod," a reminder that we should show consideration for those who had invited us. We were not to overstay. She expected us to leave within a reasonable time and that meant not being the last to leave, or even, among the last to leave.

A classic illustration she sometimes used to impress upon us the importance of sharing and not being stingy, was: "Go to the seashore and fill both hands with sand. Close one hand tightly and leave the other open. When you open the closed hand, you will find that it has less sand than the hand which remained open."

This somewhat paradoxical illustration highlighted the negative result of being tight-fisted and the value of open-handedness. It was a way of stimulating our desire to be kind and willing to share, being mindful that the good things which come to us - other people as well - are God's gifts to be used not merely for ourselves - or themselves - but also for others.

Another of Ma's important guidelines to living was not to covet what others have. Exemplifying this belief began for each of us with learning to be satisfied with what we had. According to her, when things are down with a person, that person does not have to bemoan the condition, or to complain and explain to others. Drawing from the local situation, she made this point as follows: "If you only have salt and cassava, eat that and be thankful to God. Make no complaint." People will not know what your circumstance is if you do not complain. Moreover, over time and through honest labor, your situation can be changed for the better.

When it came to discipline, Ma was strict. However, she believed, as did Pa, that the objective for each child was self-discipline. Each child was to learn what is right and what is wrong, as that child grew and developed, based on Christian principles which were the foundation stones of what was taught in the home by them. A course of action was to be determined by the dictates of our conscience and not whether someone was watching and seeing what we were doing, or someone, a friend or superior for example, had said it should be done. Sometimes, to choose to do what was right would be difficult but that should nevertheless be our choice. We needed to pray to God for assistance to make the right choice and the necessary support would come. She herself had to pray for courage to do the hard right. As Henry put it in his tribute to her referred to earlier, she prayed for strength to do the hard right as against the easy wrong; for courage to hold to your honest convictions as against the sacrifices of principles for expediency or gain; for contentment with your honest lot as against the intrigues of the lure of wealth.

In keeping with their joint efforts to bring us up, my father also tried to impress on us that choosing what was right could be difficult, but nevertheless was what should be done, even at a critical time in an individual's life. A favorite hymn of his, words by J. R. Lowell, was "Once To Every Man and Nation." Here are the opening words of this song which has stood out in my mind and been a guiding force at some of the critical times in my life: Once to every man and nation comes the moment to decide, in the strife of truth with falsehood, for the good or evil side . . .

Indeed, it is a strife which goes on forever and it is not easy to side with truth when, as the author states later in the song, hers is a "wretched crust." Yet, it is then, as he goes on, that the brave man chooses while the "coward stands aside." But ever confident one can be that even when evil prospers, wrong is on the throne, and truth on the scaffold, truth will win. To use the words of the song, "Yet that scaffold sways the future, And, behind the dim unknown, Standeth God within the shadow Keeping watch above his own."

For Ma, marriage and the family were important in the life of each individual. Marriage helped the individual to develop a sense of responsibility, provided for a stable relationship and contributed to a sense of security. It also provided for individuals to carry out sexual activity, which was a normal aspect of maturity, within the bounds of morality and dignity.

Given these beliefs, naturally she was concerned when it seemed that Henry was settling into bachelorhood. But, the situation went beyond concern when a problem developed in the home - the pregnancy of Gladys, Henry being the person responsible. She and Pa were disturbed and worried. Their obligations to him and to Gladys also made resolution of this problem and decision regarding the child painful and difficult. More so, because the sanctity of the home was violated. Henry's acknowledgment of responsibility and apologies were the first steps in the process of resolving this difficult situation.

The importance of the family was riveted in the mind of my mother from her girlhood days. In the home of her foster mother where she grew up, the strength of family ties was evident. Then, there was the reinforcement of her family of consanguinity from the time she was discovered in Edina and especially when the opportunity presented itself when she married and came to Monrovia, nearer where her consanguinal relatives lived. On her marriage to my father, she was warmly received into and embraced by his family. This relationship of warmth was mutual, enjoyed throughout her lifetime. She and my father gave family a significant place in the family established by their marriage.

Family meant love and warmth, affection and caring, work and relaxation, joy and sadness. Family, true to the African way of life, was indeed a security net from birth until death.

Work was another virtue stressed by Ma. For her, work was a normal part of day-to-day living and she felt it should be for everyone. She tried to develop in each of us a positive attitude to work. She kept busy, working and involving all of the children in the work of the home. Work was a means of learning and producing. It gave satisfaction and pleasure and provided a sense of accomplishment, dignity and worth. Not only was everyone to be involved in work but everyone was to learn to work cheerfully. She did not allow us to grumble and be cross while working. She set the example, talking, joking and teaching, as she worked, not merely about the tasks at hand, but also skills, such as organization for work and simple guidelines for living. Conversation and instruction flowed so imperceptibly into each other the difference was not easily discerned.

On the other hand, she discouraged laziness. She did so, most of the time, by making fun of laziness and joking rather than by scolding. For example, at times, when she felt one of us was being lazy, she might simply call out to that person, "don't be so L - A - Z - Y ('smart')."   Or she might talk about the "lazy man's load," and advise to avoid carrying it. For example, in the days before we had electric lights, I recall when I was responsible for all the lamps and lanterns in the home - filling them with kerosene, trimming their wicks, cleaning their shades and putting them in the appropriate places ready to be used. Well, I tried to move as many as possible on each trip from upstairs to the point downstairs where they had to be fixed and back, saving steps, I thought. Whenever a load seemed unsafe to her, she would warn against the "lazy man's load" -- the load not safe to carry. There were other times when she told funny stories about laziness. One of these stories related to a man who was so lazy that the people decided that he could not live in their town. They put him in a cart and were driving him out of the town to have him killed. On the way, they came across a group of people having a feast. They stopped and the people offered the man food. Guess what? He wanted to know if the food had been chewed. So, he asked, "Is it chawed?" When the people replied no, he simply said to those carrying him, "well, drive along." Speaking in paradoxical terms was yet another way of drawing attention to laziness. A common expression of hers was: "You are looking for work and praying to God not to find it."

My mother felt children should learn to use their minds and their hands. She spurned the practice that some of the élite families had of making a distinction in work between their own children and the children who became a part of their family, only the latter doing the menial work. This practice she referred to as "giving other people's children hands and feet and taking them from your own children," and she said it was funny to do so - I guess she really meant foolish.

She was, of course, targeting the dependence this led to, but she was not oblivious to the other messages this practice sent in a society where book knowledge was increasingly extolled and work with the hands looked down upon. For example, those children exempted from menial work could easily develop a false sense of superiority as those relegated to it developed an inferiority complex. The resulting arrogant behavior of those who felt superior she detested. In fact, she could not stand arrogance and "showing off" whether because of this practice or because, as she sometimes felt, that it was due to a person not being accustomed to good things. She described such behavior as "jackass airs" and drew it to our attention in her words of warning: "Don't put on 'jackass airs' like the peacock."

One of the things which impressed Zoe was the keen sense of time for work which Ma exhibited. In her account referred to earlier, Zoe states that she felt that tasks to be carried out had to be started early in the morning so that something worthwhile would be accomplished by noon, which marked the halfway point in the day in our tropical climate. As Zoe remembers, her explanation was that if the time is idled away, noon could go by unnoticed and before one was aware, it would be four in the afternoon and the day would draw to a close without anything worthwhile being accomplished. Such loss of time could add up to weeks, months and even years. The important messages for us were that time was precious and should not be wasted and also that it was important to try to accomplish something each day. For one thing, accomplishment gave a feeling of satisfaction. Related also was the belief of the old folks that it was not good to be idle. A common expression which they used was: "An idle hand is the devil's workshop."

Ma also encouraged us to learn well whatever we were exposed to and emphasized that whatever we set out to do should be done to the best of our ability. One's best was for her an important standard of measurement. In her words, "When you do your best, no more is required."

Doing one's best applies, of course, to whatever one is given as a responsibility to be discharged, but it also suggests identifying in a given situation what needs to be done that one is capable of doing and discharging that task to the best of one's ability.

Accountability was another value my mother stressed. It required distinguishing between what is entrusted to the care of a person and what belongs to that person. For example, if one of us was sent to carry out a financial transaction such as paying school fees, buying books and school supplies, or buying food in the market, that child was required to show what was purchased and what was spent for the things purchased and to return the correct change. Thus, each of us learned to be exact and straightforward when handling money entrusted to us, however small the amount entrusted was. What belonged to a child was what was given to him or her or earned by the child. In this connection, she drove home the idea that money should not be gotten by cheating or stealing. Her words of reminder were simply: "All money is not good money."

Accountability went, however, beyond money to other things entrusted to a person's care. The same guideline applied. Know what is yours and account for everything else to the person who owns or is responsible for those things.

Ma detested rude behavior. An example of such behavior was that which usually accompanied excessive drinking. During World War II, one of the posts at which the American soldiers were stationed when they came to Monrovia was on a hill where the lighthouse for the city was a short distance from our home. Weekend evenings especially seemed to be the time for relaxation and entertainment. Once the drinking and carousing started, we could hear the noise from her room window and other rooms on the side of the house in the direction of the lighthouse and she would sometimes say to me, "Mary Antoinette, there is jollification in the camp tonight." Then, she would add: "Liquor in, wits out"

Circumspection - yes, my mother encouraged us to be observant and fully cognizant of as much as possible in a situation, especially when the situation is difficult. Everything observed did not have to be talked about, though it should all be taken into consideration when a decision had to be made or a course of action decided upon. In her words, "See and don't see."

As to her love for our country, it was always manifest. So was her pride in the country. She had watched many interesting developments and seen many steps made to progress, as she was at the center of national life for a brief period during her girlhood and a lot during her womanhood. Ever conscious she was of the sacrifices her husband made during the nation's crisis of the 1930s and his contributions to preserving the nation's sovereignty. She had full knowledge of his subsequent efforts in the welfare of the nation and its people. It was quite natural, therefore, for her to encourage all of us to participate with pride in the various activities the schools and different organizations held from time to time to celebrate national holidays. Moreover, she stimulated our pride in our nation's institutions and made us mindful of the need to use these institutions. Using them was one way to value them and help them develop. In this connection, one institution she sometimes pointed to was Liberia College, which, for a number of years, was the only institution of higher learning in the country. Whenever there were attempts to downplay the effectiveness of the institution, she would counter that Liberia College had equipped Louis and Eddie, as she called them, to compete successfully on the international scene in the welfare of the country. That spoke volumes for the institution's quality and value and she always encouraged us to attend the institution and apply ourselves to our studies there.

We children were afraid of the dark and the dead. I recall how hearing of a death in the community literally sent shivers down our spines. It did us good to see how our parents were unmoved by either. They were not afraid of darkness or death. One way Pa showed this was walking us at night on several occasions through the Monrovia Cemetery. In the days of the mid-1930s when cars were few and far between and people had to walk most of the time, there was a short-cut path to our house from places like the Fairs Ground (later Barclay Training Center), where we went to see the national agricultural and industrial fair produced in January, 1936 and witness other events held during this period. Pa sometimes chose this path both to save time and to help us realize we had no reason to be afraid of the dead. As for Ma, I have vivid memories of her sitting alone on the upstairs porch of our house in darkness, whether or not there was news of a death in our community. Sometimes, she would be humming and sometimes simply being quiet. She would tell us not to be afraid of the dead. In her words," The dead have no power."

Rather, a death or funeral in the community served as a reminder that death is a physical separation that we will all experience. You would hear her simply say: ". . . the end of us all."

This sobering remark drives home the fact that no one escapes death. Everyone has to die. The great leveler, death makes us all equal. This brings us back to and causes us to reflect on our relationship with God, our Creator, who reigns over all and on whom each person depends. With Him at the center of our lives, life is more than day-to-day living. It has meaning and purpose.

CHAPTER 8

A Treasure Taken Away

The understanding, love and warmth that characterized the marriage of my parents grew with each passing year. Each of them considered the other God's precious gift and gave praise for that gift. They enjoyed each other's company and became dependent in different ways upon one another.

Ma kept relatively good health for most of her life, the nausea and vomiting she experienced throughout each pregnancy aside. Her main health problem, diabetes, surfaced in 1949, after the death of Pa. He was more inclined to illness. A major problem from which he suffered was high blood pressure, a condition which was exacerbated by the strains he experienced during Liberia's crisis with the League of Nations in the early 1930s. While he was in Geneva, it was necessary for him to receive medication for this and for problems resulting from the high blood pressure, one being trouble with his eyes. He continued to receive medication after his return home and the high blood pressure was kept under control. He enjoyed relatively good health for the remaining years of the 1930s and the early years of the 1940s.

Through much of this period, he was involved in reforming the nation's judicial system. Many of the reforms were stimulated by the League of Nations' Plan of Assistance, a plan resulting from a request by the Liberian Government for assistance to carry out reforms after the League of Nations Commission of Inquiry made its report in 1930. This report triggered internal problems in the country and the crisis at the League of Nations. The League's Plan evolved after a considerable period of negotiation between Liberia and the League. It was based on the report of the League's Commission of Inquiry, observations of a League Committee of Experts subsequently sent into the country and the position of the Liberian Government, reflected in its own Plan of Reforms and the observations of its representatives to the League. Also critical to evolving the Plan was the Committee of the League's Council which was appointed to study the Liberian problem. This Committee weighed the different viewpoints as well as the ideas advanced by its members. Liberia's principal representatives - my father and Antoine Sottile - made sure that the Plan evolved by the League did not compromise Liberia's sovereignty and that Liberians with the requisite expertise would be involved in implementing the Plan.

Following a successful defense of Liberia at the League of Nations, on Dec. 15, 1933, my father was appointed Chief Justice of the Supreme Court of Liberia. It was in this capacity that he had responsibility for the oversight of reforms within the Judiciary and restoring national and international confidence in the nation's Judiciary, which had eroded over the last few years.

By 1945, after about 11 and half years of work as Chief Justice, his health began to fail. Sometime around early June, 1945, his blood pressure rose so high that he began having acute problems with one of his eyes. It was necessary for him to take a leave of absence from his work and travel abroad for medical treatment. Given the level of his blood pressure, his doctor did not feel that he could survive a long air flight and so recommended that he seek medical treatment in Europe rather than in the United States.

Portugal seemed a logical place largely because of its easy access, its capital, Lisbon, being a regular stop at that time for air flights from Liberia to the United States. Also, the Allies had just won victory in Europe, ending the European phase of World War II and things were only beginning to return to normal in Europe, so options for travel and choice of a place for treatment in Europe were limited. Accordingly, he traveled to Lisbon June of 1945 and spent a few weeks there. Although his health condition seemed to have improved with treatment in Lisbon, there was a language problem as he did not speak Portuguese and he was not satisfied. He had an inquiring mind and he simply was not at ease. Not only was he unable to communicate with his doctor as he wanted to, but also he felt that he could not understand the doctor's actual assessment of his condition and, consequently, the doctor's response to his condition through medication.

It became clear to him that he needed to be in an English-speaking country. He, therefore, took advantage of the first available ship, although it was a cargo ship which could carry only a few passengers and traveled to the United States. He left Lisbon July 5 and arrived in the United States at Philadelphia, July 18. Two days later, he traveled to Washington, D.C. There he made his base in this capital city where segregation was still legal. While there, he lived in Carver Hall on the Howard University Campus and began treatment complementary to that which he had taken in Lisbon.

His overall condition improved, but the problem with his affected eye persisted, so a retinal picture had to be taken. The picture revealed that there had been a rupture of a blood vessel in the eyeball of that eye. Additional treatment followed for this problem.

At home, my mother waited with us, with concern, as he received treatment. There was also concern about his health condition among his American friends in the Washington, D.C. area, among them, Mrs. Marion Seymour and Mrs. Mabel Staupers, both professional nurses with wide contacts[37] and a few others of West Indian descent. Through these friends, he established contact with Dr. S. Aubrey Gittens, a reputable physician of West Indian descent, who resided and practiced in New York City. He proceeded there and was under the care of Dr. Gittens, who referred him for specialized treatment as needed. In New York City, his treatment continued, with relative success.

After about a couple of months in the United States, he returned home greatly improved in his overall health condition. However, he had to use a magnifying glass to read, because the damage to the affected eye was not fully ame-liorated. He returned to work and led a practically normal life for what, he and my mother did not realize, would be the last years of his life. His return, fortu-nately, almost coincided with the end of World War II and better days in Liberia. Within this period, he was able to enjoy the success the children (their own and those they were fostering) were experiencing, which included the travel abroad of both Rudolph and me for further studies.

On the day I sailed for the United States by a ship of Farrell Lines, Sept. 1, 1948, Pa visited with Aunty Mai who had not favored my travel abroad. She asked him if he was satisfied that I had left and was surprised that his answer was not only a "yes," but also that he added the words, "my life work is over." This response left her wondering whether her brother felt he was going to die some-time soon. Interestingly, there was another happening around this time which also left her and the family wondering. Ma had a strange dream. In the dream, she lost her jewelry box. She was struck that the loss was not a single piece of jewelry or several pieces of jewelry, but the entire jewelry box -- a treasure. Pa interpreted the dream, indicating that he was the jewelry box. Another premoni-tion of the death of a loved one?

Well, there was hardly time to ponder the dream for, in early December, 1948, illness struck. Pa suffered a stroke which resulted in a paralysis of the left side and the loss of his sight. For nearly two weeks, doctors fought, Ma and the closest members of the family at his bedside, except Rudolph and me, who were in the United States. It was all in vain. He did not recover. Three months to the date of my arrival in the United States, at home, on the morning of Dec. 14, he succumbed to death at the age of 65. Ma's treasure was taken away by death. What a blow for her, all of us children and the rest of the family!

CHAPTER 9

Adjusting to Life Without Louis

Losing a spouse is like losing a part of your very self. So it was with my mother. Part of her literally died when her beloved Louis died. Her life was so much wrapped up in his that it took her a long time to adjust to his death. This being the biggest loss of a loved one which she had sustained, she spent much time weeping and mourning. She went into deep black (custom of wearing exclusively black garments and no jewelry), mourning her loss, in keeping with the custom in Liberia at the time. An inkling of how she felt, however, was the fact that she went beyond custom, remaining in deep black months longer than the one year widows in Liberia customarily mourned in deep black at that time. But for my wedding which took place about four months before the second anniversary of my father's death, there is no telling how long she would have continued in deep mourning. The wedding was, however, an occasion for rejoicing and celebration. She had to savor the joy of this occasion for my father and herself, the first big event since her marriage that she would be celebrating without him. Aunty Mai and other close relatives and friends convinced her that she had to come out of black.

Henry and the foster children who watched the state into which she sank as a result of our father's death did everything to console her. They were concerned about her, as were those of her own children and the foster children who were not living in close proximity at the time. Henry in particular gave up a lot of his leisure time activities to be with her. All of the children wondered whether she would recover from this loss and find a new life for herself.

In this period of deep sadness, fortunately she had her Christian faith to rely on. She reminded herself that whatever God ordains is right. She also reminded herself of God's promise to the fatherless and widows. Having long ago lost her parents and foster parents, she was now also a widow. She would: "Hold God to His promises."

She paused and counted her blessings, beginning with the fact that God had given her a loving and devoted husband for 37 years. They had had a happy marriage and together had made significant marks in life. All of their own children were grown and were proving themselves successful in their endeavors. She was blessed too that the majority of the children who had become a part of the family they had established were leading successful lives. Moreover, she had been at her husband's bedside throughout his illness and done for him all she could. Her being there meant a lot to him and to herself. Besides, long before his illness, he had expressed the wish that he would not outlive her. His death had come rather early, but she faced the future assured that God would be with her in this new stage in her life as he had been with her from her birth.

On the horizon was my forthcoming marriage. It would be a major first step in lifting the gloom into which she had sunk, as planning for it would soon have to begin. There was much to be done and she was elated. I was bestowing pride on the family and she would marry me off with the pomp and grandeur befitting such an occasion, as her foster mother had married her off some 37 years before. Yes, planning for my wedding would force my mother to focus on a significant event and happy occasion.

However, before planning for the wedding got underway, Ma experienced a problem which necessitated added focus on herself. She suffered a wound in her foot which was extremely difficult to heal. The medical check showed that this was caused by her having developed diabetes. Naturally, there was the fight first to get the wound healed, the diagnosis being a 50-50 chance of healing without amputation of the affected foot. She was alarmed and fretful to hear about the possibility of amputation and was strongly against it. Henry, who was on the spot, decided to go along with her and take the chance of treatment rather than amputation. It was a big chance, but with the blessing of God, it worked! She was treated for some time by Dr. Arthur Schnitzer, the family doctor, and the wound healed. The next step was to ensure regular medication to keep the diabetes under control. The regimen included a daily injection of insulin which had to be given by a professional nurse. Ma realized as time went by that this aspect of the regimen would continue for time indefinite and she wished more and more to learn how to give herself the insulin injection. She simply did not want to have to depend on a nurse coming in daily. She looked forward to the day she would learn how to do this for herself.

Meanwhile, in October, 1949, I returned home with the degree of Master of Arts in Teaching from Radcliffe College. Having been abroad more than a year, it was wonderful to have me back. She was proud of me for my accomplishment. Also, I would be good company for her. My arrival shifted her focus. Shortly after, she began planning for my wedding and got increasingly involved in that.

The wedding was held Aug. 2, 1950 at Trinity Pro-Cathedral (formerly Trinity Memorial Church and since the mid-1960s Trinity Cathedral), the Rev. W. O. Davies-Jones, Rector officiating. The wedding reception was held at our home- the home into which she and Pa moved into in December, 1912, one year after their marriage. Suggestions that the wedding reception be held at the then recently built Executive Pavilion which had begun to be let out for private functions were not accepted by her. She had every good reason to use our home and not a public place. Five hundred invitations were sent out and Ma knew that she could expect a good response to the invitations and some additional people too, for, in Liberia at the time, weddings were not closed affairs when held by people well known in the community. So, she planned accordingly and the reception was held both in the house and outside in the flower garden she had cultivated over the years.

Kedrick Wellington Brown, the groom, was well known to the Grimes family. He was the son of Dixon Byrd Brown, a Liberian and a very close friend of Pa and Angeline Wallace, a Sierra Leonean. In fact, he was my father's Godson. Ma felt confident that the wedding would be blessed and would last until he and I were separated by death, as had occurred with her and Pa.

At the time of the wedding, Kedrick was working in the private sector, his position, Assistant Cashier at the Bank of Monrovia in Monrovia where he was acting as Cashier. He had worked in banking for a number of years, beginning as a teller at the Bank of Monrovia and then, in various positions at the State Bank of Ethiopia in Addis Ababa, where he had worked his way up to Branch Manager. Since July, 1947, he had returned to the Bank of Monrovia and become the first Liberian to be appointed an Officer in this Bank.

About a month after the wedding, Kedrick was appointed Financial Attaché to the Liberian Embassy in Washington, D.C., United States. He accepted the appointment and took off for his post in early September, leaving me behind to close out our business which included leasing of the house on Carey Street, Snapper Hill, which he had completed and moved into about a month before our wedding and which had been our home since the wedding. With me for a while were his mother and sister, Marilyn Sawyerr, who had come from Sierra Leone, with Marilyn's toddler, Kedrick Sawyer, for the wedding.

How nice it would be if our mother accompanied me whenever I left to join Kedrick, Henry thought! This would give her a chance to change her surroundings and improve her emotional state, as she continued to adjust to life without our father. It would also provide the opportunity for her to get specialized help in solving her health problems. Kedrick and I welcomed the idea, but it took a lot of persuading and coaxing to get Ma to agree to it. For one thing, Liberian women of her generation hardly ever traveled out of the country. To begin with, very few people had the money for travel to foreign parts. Besides, women were immersed in taking care of their husbands and in having and rearing their own children as well as the children they and their husbands were fostering. These tasks just about occupied their lifetime, given the relatively short life span of people in Liberia at that time. In my mother's case, she was blessed to have already entered her 60s. However, up to that point, she had traveled out of the country only once. The trip was literally next door, to Freetown, Sierra Leone, during the 1920s when she was part of the entourage of President King and his wife, Adeline. Henry pointed out to her that life was now different. Our father was gone. Her own children and practically all of the foster children were grown. She needed to concentrate on herself.

With her conceding this, planning for the trip began, a trip which would prove beneficial to her health and her overall adjustment. In addition to receiving specialized attention for her health problems, there was opportunity for a much needed change and for relaxation. New scenes, new experiences and new contacts, as well as old ties renewed, provided long-lasting stimulation.

A first step in the planning was a decision regarding where she would seek medical attention. Dr. Hildrus Poindexter, then Chief of the United States Public Health Mission to Liberia and a friend of the family, recommended that she go for treatment and management of her diabetes to the Deaconess Hospital in Boston, Massachusetts. He knew that there Dr. Elliott Joslin had pioneered a striking approach in the care and treatment of persons suffering from diabetes. With Dr. Poindexter's assistance, the necessary contact was made.

Around the end of March, 1951, she and I sailed for the United States via Europe. We traveled on one of the Dutch mail boats which plied the West African coast, the "Maaskerk." The ship accommodated 66 passengers and it was at its capacity. It was pleasant for us to have among the passengers Alford Russ (son of Emma Alberta Morgan Russ, a first cousin of Pa who grew up in Grand Bassa County and her husband Alford Russ),[38] his wife, Iola; and their only child, a teenage son, whose name was Louis.

Ma thoroughly enjoyed the sailing. Having lived near the ocean during her years of growing up in Edina and her period of study in Harper, the ocean conjured pleasant memories. Moreover, there was a lot to do aboard the ship for enjoyment and relaxation throughout the sailing.

The ship made its regular stops on the West African coast - Freetown and Dakar - and then went to Las Palmas, Canary Islands, where we went ashore and did some sightseeing. Our first stop in Europe was a brief one - at Dover, England, near our destination. Only disembarking passengers were allowed to go ashore there. Nevertheless, the stop provided a splendid opportunity for us to view the "white cliffs of Dover." Our next stop was Rotterdam, Holland, where we and all other remaining passengers disembarked. There was a lot to attract attention in Rotterdam. That was also the case in Amsterdam and other parts of Holland to which we traveled; in Switzerland; and in France where we visited also.

Most of the time was spent in Holland. After sightseeing in Rotterdam where we landed, we visited Amsterdam and The Hague and traveled in the countryside between Haarlem and Leiden where the flower fields predominate. On landing in Rotterdam, a feeling of sadness engulfed us as we saw the scars from the massive destruction this important port suffered as a result of the bombs dropped by the Germans on the city's center during World War II. These were grim reminders of that War which ended a few years earlier. Otherwise, the notes were pleasant. It was the beginning of spring on the continent and the season in Holland when the bulbs were in bloom. Ma loved flowers and she was thrilled to see the tulips and other flowers in bloom; so was I. The country was literally carpeted with flowers. The flowers, the lowlands and water everywhere combined to make a landscape that was picturesque and striking. The experience was memorable for us.

In Switzerland, the visit was to Geneva. This was another example of natural beauty and picturesque scenery. The mountainous terrain, with snow-capped mountains, presented scenery of indescribable beauty. In addition, in Geneva, there were two sentimental notes. We had the opportunity of visiting the

Palais du Nations, headquarters of the League of Nations, where Pa had spent much time during the 1930s in the defense of our country. We also visited with Estelle Brown, Kedrick's youngest sibling, who was then studying at the University of Geneva.

In France, there was a short stop in Paris. We visited there with Florence Sherman Peal (daughter of Lizzie Barclay Sherman and Reginald Sherman) and her husband, Edward Peal, then First Secretary of the Liberian Legation and their two little children, Allen and Rhoda, and went sightseeing. Then, it was travel to Le Havre and boarding the luxury liner, Ile de France, for the Atlantic Ocean crossing to New York.

We thoroughly enjoyed the few days aboard the Ile de France. Blessed with calm seas, we spent a lot of time relaxing on deck and enjoying the ocean in its serenity and with all the awe it inspires. Then there were the grandeur and splendor of life on board. There was so much to do - dining, dancing, games, movies - everything in the elegance and style characteristic of such luxury liners. One of the things my mother relished was the early morning tea served while in bed. It gave her a feeling of being pampered. For me who was not the early morning riser like she was, it was what I liked to style, the "awakening tea," something I preferred to skip and sleep. This preference of mine aside, we both found the trip fascinating and we were left with pleasant memories which remained with us for a long time.

We arrived in New York City to a warm welcome from Kedrick, who had driven up from Washington, D.C., and from Rudolph, who accompanied Kedrick. Rudolph was then based in New York City, completing graduate studies at Columbia University. After clearing the immigration formalities, we were driven to Washington, D.C., to the home Kedrick had established. Here my mother would spend an enjoyable eight months with Kedrick and me, traveling on occasion to New York City, Boston and Atlanta.

Our arrival in Washington, D.C., coincided with the blossoming of the cherry trees, an attraction for residents of the area and visitors. The picturesque scenery the cherry blossoms presented and the sweet fragrance reminded us of what we had recently experienced during the tulip season in Holland. It was indeed delightful for us. Moreover, from her reading, my mother knew the story of the cherry blossoms - Japan's gift to the United States - so they were a special attraction for her. They provided a pleasant atmosphere within the Tidal Basin area to view the historic landmarks - the Washington Monument, the Lincoln Memorial and the Jefferson Memorial.

There were several high points to Ma's stay in the United States. The first of these was her attending, accompanied by Kedrick and me, the 1951 Commencement Convocation of Columbia University, New York City. It was during this Convocation that Rudolph received the degree of Master of International Affairs. It was a thrilling experience for us all, especially for her, as she had not been able to attend the 1949 Commencement Convocation of Harvard University when Rudolph received the LL.B degree (now J.D. degree). She was proud of him for the double scholastic achievement he had attained in a little more than four years in the United States.

He would return home and build a distinguished career in the Liberian Foreign Service, becoming Secretary of State in 1960 and enjoying the distinction of being our nation's longest serving Secretary of State in terms of consecutive years of service. Among important developments during his tenure as Secretary of State was the formation of the Organization of African Unity (OAU), Liberia playing a significant role in the organizational process. His contributions to the OAU were invaluable, two of these being, his drafting of the English text of the OAU Charter and his participation in presenting the case against Portugal and South Africa at the United Nations, one of the four African Ministers selected by the OAU Heads of State to perform this task. Prior to his becoming Secretary of State, in 1954, he organized the Law School at the University of Liberia, which was named after our father, Louis Arthur Grimes. This made possible for the first time formal studies in the country in Law and replaced apprenticeship training as the sole means of preparing for a legal career.

Another high point of Ma's stay in the United States was her meeting Mrs. Marion Seymour and Mrs. Mabel Staupers, friends of the family, who lived in Washington, D.C. She shared many pleasant moments with them, especially with Mrs. Seymour, for whom she literally became a traveling companion. They visited several places in Washington, D.C., and attended a number of socials. They also traveled out of Washington, D.C. A memorable visit was to Atlanta, Georgia; where they witnessed Mrs. Staupers receive the Spingarn Medal for her successful work in the integration of African-American nurses into the mainstream of American nursing, having led the fight for 15 years (1934-1949) in her capacity of Executive Secretary of the National Association of Colored Graduate Nurses (NACGN). In addition to this important ceremony, she enjoyed sightseeing in Atlanta. There she got a feel for what African-Americans had been able to accomplish in the still segregated Deep South. It was a surprise to her to see what positive response they had made to this environment and she was deeply impressed. She noted with pride the outstanding achievements they had made in professional and other areas of life and the quality homes they owned which contributed to the beauty of the city.

In Washington, D.C., she also had the privilege of meeting and visiting with Mrs. Mary Church Terrell, a long-time activist in the struggle for equal rights for African-Americans. She marveled at the fact that although Mrs. Terrell was then in her 80s, she was still active in the struggles to abolish segregation in Washington, D.C. and throughout the country. Mrs. Terrell's commitment to this cause was evident and my mother was impressed. Of course, she knew that segregation existed in the United States before her visit to the country, but Washington, D.C., afforded her the opportunity to get some ideas first hand of segregation and its evils, for segregation was still alive and well in this capital city of the United States. She could appreciate the fight of Mrs. Terrell and others against segregation.

Ma began taking care of her health problems with dental work in Washington, D.C. The really big experience was, however, becoming a patient of Dr. Elliot Joslin at the Deaconess Hospital in Boston. The approach pioneered by Dr. Joslin in dealing with diabetics was exactly what she needed and wanted. It consisted not only of treatment to control the disease but also opportunities for each diabetic to understand what the disease really was and to learn how to take care of himself/herself. She responded enthusiastically to this approach and readily provided the cooperation expected of patients.

Hospitalized for about a week at the Deaconess Hospital, her body metabolism was studied and a diet designed to suit her needs. This meant that she did not have to resort to eating "diabetic foods," but instead could use the diet guide prepared especially for her to plan her own meals, drawing from foods regularly eaten by people without diabetes and other health problems. While in the hospital, she attended the daily classes for patients. In them, she learned a lot about diabetes and what she could do to help keep her diabetes under control. This included recognizing the importance of diet and of adhering to the main features of the diet worked out for her; learning how to give herself insulin injections; understanding what insulin shock was and how to avoid it, its dangers and how to overcome it should it be experienced; things to do to minimize - in fact, prevent the chances of diabetic coma. She learned also how to test urine and determine whether it was positive or negative and how to use this information to decide when it was necessary to consult a doctor. As relatives and interested persons could attend the classes with the patient, I attended the classes with her. The valuable information gained stood her in good stead for the rest of her life and provided awareness for me and other members of the family which was very useful. For the approximately 19 more years thereafter that she lived, she was blessed to have suffered none of the side effects of diabetes such as eye trouble, which often leads to blindness, or incurable sores which often result in amputation of limbs. Her contribution to her success in this endeavor was due both to the knowledge she had acquired and to her will power to adhere to her diet and the other aspects of her regimen. She had a "sweet tooth," so the part her will power played in the successful management of her diabetes cannot be overstated.

Before leaving Boston, accompanied by me, Ma had the interesting experience of visiting with and renewing her acquaintance with Mrs. Harriet Wharton, who was then living in the Boston area with the younger three of her four children and her mother. She and her husband were then divorced. Mrs. Wharton was a friend of hers from the 1920s when Mrs. Wharton was residing in Monrovia with her husband, Clifton R. Wharton, then Third Secretary in the United States Legation (now United States Embassy) there. It was a really pleasant reunion. They spent a lot of time reminiscing and each brought the other up-to-date on significant events that had transpired in their respective lives. I felt, as they talked, that the closeness they had for each other had endured.

On her return to Washington, D.C., Ma began right away to put what she had learned into practice and to become proficient in doing so. It was a joy for me to work with her on ensuring that her diet was in keeping with the guidelines worked out for her by the Deaconess Hospital. I admired her desire to adhere to her diet and the tremendous will power she exhibited toward achieving this end. She had a lot to claim her attention and time slipped by. Soon, fall began to set in, with the beautiful colors of the foliage and, yes, the cold weather! We could see that she did not like the cold weather. Although she was enjoying her stay, she made it clear to Kedrick and me that she did not want the winter to meet her in the United States. Her thoughts started turning homeward. Accordingly, we began the necessary arrangements so that she could return home before the beginning of the winter.

Meanwhile, in Monrovia, Henry was having some basic changes made to the home that would give it less of the familiar look it had up to the time of our father's death. Simultaneously, he was introducing some modern features into the structure that would make living easier. These changes would also help her adjustment to her new life.

In early December, she set sail for home, traveling on a ship of Farrell Lines, bound for Monrovia from New York. This ship, like the others of this company and the ships of other companies that plied directly between the United States and Liberia, was a cargo vessel that carried only 12 passengers. It was quite a contrast to the luxury liner she and I had traveled by to the United States from France. Aboard was one of her Godchildren, John Coleman - son of long-time friends, David Coleman and Etta Coleman. John was returning home, having completed studies with a major in civil engineering. She had watched him grow up and was very proud of him for his general demeanor, his scholastic and other attainments. He was good company for her and she was pleased that he had decided to return home to contribute to our country in an area of expertise in which qualified Liberians were few.

After about two weeks of sailing, she arrived home to a warm welcome from Henry; Rudolph, who returned home from the United States about a couple of months before her; the foster children; Aunty Mai; Aunty Pai; other relatives; friends; and well-wishers. Psychologically and physically, she was prepared for the new phase in her life into which Pa's death had ushered her. Gradually, she settled into this new life.

Among the special happenings of this period was the arrival of five of her grandchildren, changing the total from one in a period of 10 years to six. This was quite a growth in the new generation that was springing from her direct line and she had a number of young children with whom to become involved and enjoy. For her, it was a splendid opportunity and she considered herself blessed.

Meanwhile, there were high points in this period which she had looked forward to - the marriages of Henry and Rudolph and of two of the children in the extended family, George and Lottie. Henry's marriage took place in Monrovia on March 6, 1955. He married Euphemia Reeves, daughter of Jude Reeves and Juah (nickname Joy) Reeves and foster granddaughter of Cousin Eddie and Cousin Phemie. A few months earlier, on Oct. 31, 1954, Rudolph married Doris Duncan, daughter of Henry B. Duncan and Nancy Martin. The wedding took place in New York City. Doris was then completing her studies for the Master's degree in Economics at New York University. The day was especially significant as they were both born on Oct. 31, albeit different years. George married on Oct. 5, 1955 in Monrovia, to Maude Fagans, daughter of Margaret Robertson and stepdaughter of Frederick D. Robertson, Maude's father, Albert Jerome Fagans having predeceased her mother when she was very little. Almost 10 months later, on July 29, 1956, in Monrovia, Lottie married Thomas Johnson, a 1949 graduate of Liberia College.

Going back to the grandchildren, the first of the lot of five, Kedrick Wellington, Jr. (nickname K.B.), was born to Kedrick and me in Washington, D.C., during July, 1952, seven months after Ma left for home. Our second, Victoria Angeline Lducia, born in New York City in April, 1955, was the next.[39] Then came the daughters of Henry, both born in Monrovia; Pearl Adalicia to Henry and Martha Holder during September, 1955 and Joy Makra to Henry and Euphemia in June, 1957. The last of the children of Kedrick and me and of this set of grandchildren, Byrd Arthur Marbue, was born in Monrovia during December, 1960.[40] We had then returned home to live.

In addition to this new phase of family life, the period was characterized by the continuation of my mother's work in the Church and in the Eastern Star, which was considered the apex of the societies for women in Liberian "sophisticated society." This sister organization of the Ancient Free and Accepted Masons shared the mystique and grandeur of the Masons. Whenever the Masons had a public procession in celebration of Masonic feast days, the laying of cornerstones for an important building and other public events in which the Masonic Craft was involved, the Eastern Star processed with the Masons. Even the meeting place for the Eastern Star was one floor of the Masonic Temple.

The requirement for membership in the Eastern Star was relationship to a Master Mason as wife, widow, sister, daughter, or mother. The Master Mason had to be in good standing at the time the person joined the Eastern Star or had been so at the time of his death. Interestingly, a Master Mason in good standing could also become a member of the Eastern Star. During the 1930s, Ma "joined on her husband," to put it commonly. That is, she took advantage of her eligibility by virtue of her husband being a Master Mason in good standing and became initiated into Queen Esther Chapter No. 1 of the Order of Eastern Star, the Chapter based in Monrovia. By the time of Pa's death, she had become Worthy Matron of the Chapter and passed the Chair, becoming a member of the Grand Chapter of the Order. Thus, her affiliation with the organization after her return home in 1951 was as a member of the Grand Chapter of the Order. She gradually rose in the Grand Chapter. In December, 1959, she was elected Grand Matron for one year, during which year, among significant events, was the groundbreaking for a new Masonic Temple on Benson Street in Monrovia. Elected Associate Grand Matron and serving with her was Mrs. Annabel Walker. They were both reelected for another year in December, 1960, despite her recommendation in her Annual

Report that she be succeeded by Mrs. Walker. After a second year of service as Grand Matron, she moved into the revered company of Past Grand Matrons.

As for the Church, it was like a lifeline for Ma. Her ties with Trinity remained firm and strong. She was regular in her attendance at worship services. Her work in the Church continued and she remained a faithful member of Trinity until her death.

Before Pa's death, her work with the Women's Auxiliary of Trinity Church had begun to extend beyond Trinity to the General Auxiliary of the Missionary Diocese of Liberia (now the Diocese of Liberia). She had become Treasurer of the General Auxiliary and United Thanks Offering (UTO) Custodian for the Missionary Diocese. In this latter capacity, she spent considerable time and energy in this new period of her life, for full participation in the UTO as a Missionary Diocese was relatively new at the time. For years, the Missionary Diocese had been a beneficiary of funds contributed by the Episcopal Church of the United States, some of it from the UTO ingathered at the Triennials of the Episcopal Church of the USA.

The UTO funds were used mainly for the Episcopal educational institutions that served girls in Liberia. The Missionary Diocese had, however, reached a stage when it did not wish to be a mere recipient from the fund but a donor to it as well. Her task was to help women in the organizations of Episcopal Church Women in the Churches throughout the Missionary Diocese grasp the significance of the fund and of the need for active participation in it, thereby stimulating their giving to it. The UTO appealed to her. It was a way of thanksgiving. It stimulated awareness of blessings, often taken for granted and linked blessings and giving. A ministry provided by the Church, individual women acknowledged on a regular basis the blessings from God they and their families received by giving, using the "Blue Box," a special box into which coins are dropped every time a woman felt she wanted to give thanks for a blessing she had received. These individual gifts were combined at the Parish level and later at the level of the Missionary Diocese at corporate communion services held periodically at specially designated times during the Church's year. The UTO ingathered from the Missionary Diocese was then sent to the Episcopal Church Center in New York where it was combined with the funds ingathered from the various Dioceses in the United States and from other parts of the world. There was some measure of success in this endeavor and this can be attributed partly to Ma's work and also to the fact that many women in the Missionary Diocese had received some part of their education in Liberia in Episcopal Church schools, especially the mission schools. They welcomed opportunities for linking individual and corporate prayers with blessings and giving and for contributing to this joint fund.

The period was an interesting one, as new voluntary associations were emerging to assist in responding to the various social welfare needs and problems that were increasing and becoming visible as a result of the changing times. Ma joined and worked with several of the new organizations, notably among them the Antoinette Tubman Children's Welfare Foundation, which was founded in 1956 and had as its concern orphan children. The formation of this organization was spearheaded by Mrs. Antoinette Tubman, wife of President William V. S. Tubman, and Mrs. Anna Locker, wife of the then American Ambassador to Liberia, Jesse Locker, who became its first President.

The Foundation set as a goal building the necessary facility and providing institutional care for orphan children from infancy to 12 years of age. Through the dedicated efforts of its members, a building was completed and furnished in 1958 and a home for orphan children opened in Virginia, situated on the St. Paul River, a few miles from Monrovia. Ma enjoyed being a part of this organization, immersing herself in its work. When Mrs. Locker had to leave Liberia before the end of her tenure as President and return home due to the unexpected death of her husband, she recommended and Ma was elected by the Foundation to succeed her as President. Thus, Ma was at the helm of the Foundation during the initial years of its work

She also connected herself with the Young Women's Christian Association (YWCA), which was revitalized in this period. She worked with the YWCA and became a member of its Board. In this capacity, she saw the YWCA acquire its own land and construct on Tubman Boulevard, Sinkor, the country's first YWCA building. This important development facilitated the extension of the work of the YWCA, especially in Monrovia.

Other new activities that marked the period for her were related to the home front in the areas of preservation of the papers of Pa and continuation of the remodeling of the home that Henry began during her absence from the country. But, it was not all work. She returned to the social life of the Monrovia high society she had known during Pa's lifetime. It was a life she enjoyed, a life in which she, now widow of a Chief Justice, was accorded the same place of respect and honor she had enjoyed while her husband was alive.

Feelings in the community about the active life she led were mixed. Some felt she was too active for a person of her age, especially on the social scene and they did not fail to communicate these feelings to us, suggesting that we restrain her. Of course, this view was fostered by people whose thinking was shallow. They felt that a person in the 60s was old and such persons should be relegated to the home and a life of relative inactivity. My mother did not pay attention to this line of thinking. She simply went on with her life. Her health and vitality rather than her age would set the limits to how active she would be. Moreover, there were those who admired and appreciated seeing her in an active role. They enjoyed sharing with her in work and in socializing with her. She threw her lot in with this latter group. To them, she was a valuable source of ideas and strength and good company. To the organizations in which she became involved, she contributed a combination of insights, experience, dedication and hard work. Worthwhile endeavors provided opportunities both for her to contribute in areas of need and for her to express herself, thereby maintaining purpose and significance in her life. As for us, we were happy to see her full of energy and life and successfully meeting the challenges of this new phase of her life.

On the home front, her activities reflected her commitment to the perpetuation of the memory of her beloved Louis and his work as well as her life with him and the family they had built. These included the preservation of the home. Her activities were also indicative of her foresight and her creativity, especially as hardly anything was being done at the time to memorialize important national figures in concrete ways, such as the preservation of their papers, of their homes, or of their important memorabilia. In fact, little was known or available in the country at the time in the area of document preservation.

As for the preservation of homes, a bigger and more costly venture, people gave no thought to such an undertaking. They may have felt helpless in view of the high cost such preservation required or may not have perceived any value in such efforts. Houses built in the past hundred years when houses were of frame rather than concrete did not survive for long the ravages of the weather and of insects. She saw several homes in her neighborhood and the larger community deteriorate and disappear and with them, many precious memories of "old times." Such losses to communities and the nation no doubt helped to spark her interest in the preservation of her husband's papers and the home they had made for their family.

Not only did she believe that preserving their home was a task she needed to undertake, she literally became obsessed with the idea and engrossed in translating it into reality. Without talk or fanfare, she set about this task, "taking her own time," to use the Liberian expression, thus spreading the cost over time. Her objective was to change as much of the house as possible from wood to concrete, while retaining to the extent possible its original form. In the process, she would add touches that would give the house some of the looks of the modern-type houses that were then being built in Monrovia. Everything was in her mind, seemingly evolving only as she progressed in the task. She, therefore, had to be her own architect. It is to her credit that she basically achieved what she set out to do by the time of her death in 1970 and that the Grimes home is a landmark on Snapper Hill of homes constructed in the early decades of the 1900s in that part of the city and in other parts of the city as well. It stood in good shape up to the Civil War of the 1990s. Fortunately, it survived that destructive War during which many homes were destroyed and still stands, although it suffered some resulting deterioration.

The home has mainly served Trinity Cathedral since Ma's death, something which would, no doubt, please her and Pa. Leased by Trinity Cathedral a few years after her death; it has served as the Deanery, first occupied by Rev. Edward G. W. King; his wife, Flossie; and their family. Thereafter, by Rev. Emmanuel Johnson, who succeeded the Rev. King; his wife, Henrietta; and their family, up to 1990. It was then that the attempt by Charles Taylor to remove, by military force, the quasi-military ruler, Samuel Kanyon Doe and overthrow his repressive regime, escalated into a civil war. Rev. Johnson was forced, with his family, to evacuate the house and flee the country. The house was then taken over and used, for the next few years, by the Economic Community of West African

States Monitoring Group (ECOMOG), the military force of ECOWAS, responsible to help end the civil strife and facilitate the country's return to constitutional rule.

The other task which claimed Ma's attention, as she carried on the repairs and remodeling of the home, related to the sorting, weeding and organizing of the papers and other effects of Pa. In this task, she got me involved. I continued this work after her death, with the assistance of my foster daughter, Hawa Turay. Our accomplishment was such that the family was able to donate a substantial portion of the papers to the University of Liberia Library. These papers became a part of the University's Africana collection under the title, "Collection of the Honorable Louis Arthur Grimes, 1883-1948." The collection has proved to be a valuable resource for researchers in Liberia. Microfilmed by African Imprint Library Service, with permission, the collection has also been made available to researchers outside of Liberia, especially in the United States and continues to serve scholars researching on Liberia.

Ma fitted these important tasks into her normal daily living and got many hours of satisfaction from them. Naturally, her belief that she was doing something worthwhile helped to propel her. She hoped that her efforts would be far-reaching but never dreamed they would be as far-reaching as time has shown, especially with regard to the papers. Donation of the collection by the family to the University of Liberia Library after her death and inquiries regarding what the University was doing in the area of document preservation sparked the interest of the University Library in this area of work and led to its first major step in the preservation of documents.

CHAPTER 10

Final Days -- "The End of us All"

A decade and a half after my mother's return home from the U.S., she was still leading an active life. Full of energy and with her characteristic zest, she had made a remarkable adjustment to this new stage in her life. Well into her 70s, she enjoyed good health and continued her work on the home front, in the Church and in the community.

She remained on Snapper Hill in what became home for her early in her marriage. Much of the time she had two paid hands - a cook, working in the home, and a watchman, working on the outside. Having spent most of her life in this home, a substantial portion of it enjoying life with her beloved Louis and involved in rearing us and the children of their extended family, she had a sentimental attachment to the home. It was filled with memories for her. Moreover, the home ensured the independence she had enjoyed over the years. She could carry on the daily routine of living and doing things much as she was accustomed to and wanted to. Then, there were the familiar surroundings of the neighborhood and neighbors she had known for years. To this home she clung for these reasons and as if doing so provided the assurance that there was where she would be laid out whenever death struck.

By the mid-1960s, when she was about 77 years of age, she experienced an inexplicable loss of weight. A medical examination showed nothing organically wrong. It seemed like a signal that the aging process had begun to set in. Henry felt that she should move in with him, Rosina,[41] whom he had then recently married, and their children in their home in Sinkor, a rapidly developing residential suburb of Monrovia. However, as much as he tried to persuade her to do so, he could not get her to make the move. Fortunately, at the time, Lottie was employed at the Government Hospital which was situated near her home. Almost everyday after work, before going home, she stopped to keep her company, see how she was coming along and find out if there was something she needed to have done. Lottie's regular and frequent visits, added to those, whenever possible, of the other children and their families, Lottie's family and other close relatives, reduced the anxiety Henry, especially, was beginning to feel.

A number of months went by before Ma began to have second thoughts about living by herself. And then, she came up with an idea of her own - encouraging me to make my home with her. I had left the country, with my three small children; Kini's daughter, Mary Victoria Hawa Freeman (called Hawa), one of my two relatives we were fostering; and my two nieces, Pearl Grimes and Joy

Grimes, in September, 1963, following the sudden death months earlier of Kedrick. My objective was to pursue advanced graduate studies in the United States. With the Doctor of Philosophy degree earned and my return expected in March, 1967 - all of the children had returned earlier - Ma proposed that I reestablish, with my children, in her home.

This idea never appealed to me. For one thing, I wanted to be away from Snapper Hill where I had grown up and also spent the 12 years of my marriage, the home of Kedrick and myself having been in the same area, although on a different street. Also, I felt that I needed to reestablish myself in a new setting, to cope with my own readjustment to life without Kedrick and to provide my children opportunities in a newly developing area of greater Monrovia. The small house Kedrick and I had completed building in Sinkor and leased out about a year before his death seemed ideal. On my request, it had been withdrawn from lease before my return home and my mother's expressed wish. Nevertheless, my children and I spent the first six months of my stay at home with her. This was to allow time for me to furnish the house in Sinkor and time, I hoped, to persuade her to join us in that home.

Meanwhile, our family and I especially, suffered a shocking loss. Within the first month of my stay home, my only daughter, Lducia, then nearly 12 years old, was hit by a car while crossing Tubman Boulevard, Sinkor, from the YWCA building to the home of Anna Sherman Richards (daughter of Lizzie Barclay Sherman and Reginald Sherman) and her husband, Joseph Richards. She died less than 48 hours after. Trying to cope with this big sadness, I felt impelled to get into a new setting. Ma shared my grief, but I was unsuccessful in getting her to move with the children and me to our Sinkor home. She continued to cling to the home she had known for more than half a century. According to her, it was there that her husband had left her. There she would stay.

All of us children were concerned about her living by herself, more so than it seems she was. So, we coaxed her to accept minor adjustments in her living arrangements and were relieved when she agreed. Moving in with her was George Molondoi Kiawoin, one of the teenage sons of Massa, one of Aunty Pai's daughters. He welcomed this mutually beneficial arrangement that allowed him to be a little closer to St. Patrick, the high school he was attending. Each evening they were joined by one of her older grandchildren, Jim or K.B., who took turns sleeping at her home. Thus, the home came alive a little more than it had been.

We also got her to agree to let the main meal of the day - lunch - be provided from one of our homes, thus reducing the cooking in her home. Naturally, the major responsibility for that fell to me and I was happy that it did. However, Rosina took over the Saturday lunch each week - fufu and soup or okra sauce, with benne seed.

Despite these arrangements, she was still by herself a lot and what we were trying to avert happened. One Saturday afternoon when she was alone in the house, she suffered an insulin shock. The day was saved by her watchman, Gbae, who from outside heard a thump on the floor. He immediately went to the door nearest to her living quarters and knocked. After waiting for some time without receiving a response from her, he went to Aunty Mai's house, a few yards down the road from hers and had a call placed to me.

I passed the information on to Henry and Rudolph by telephone and rushed to her home. It was apparent when I walked in what had happened, for her lunch was on the table, untouched. Busying herself, as she always did, it seems she had forgotten to stop and eat. But, I knew she was diligent about following the regimen for her diabetes, so I assumed that she had given herself an injection of the slow acting insulin that morning and it had been at work in her body. I promptly gave her a little sugar and called Dr. H. Nehemiah Cooper, her doctor. She revived before either he or my brothers arrived at her home. Dr. Cooper confirmed that it was an insulin shock and that I had taken the appropriate step in time. What a relief for us all!

Naturally, we were uneasy about leaving her in her home that night, although she seemed to be all right. In fact, we felt that it was the opportune time to get her into one of our homes where it was less likely that she would be alone for any long period of time. We coaxed her and she reluctantly agreed to spend just that night with me and my children. For us, that was enough. We decided, from that point, that we would simply take it one day at a time. We felt blessed when we got her to extend her stay to a week. Then, we got her to extend for another week and on until she had spent a month. From then, it was for another month and on. Meanwhile, we left everything in her house intact, including most of her clothes, as though she was living there. It worked! She remained with us for the next two years - in fact, until her death, except for brief stays in the Cooper Clinic, Sinkor, for medical attention.

Her move to us marked what turned out to be the final phase of her life. Still strong, lively and cheerful, she was good company for all of us. However, she had to face the reality of gradually giving up her attention to the preservation tasks which had for years consumed a good portion of her time. Fortunately, much had been achieved and it was not long before she found a new focus - our home, especially the children.

As might be expected, she made several trips to her home - to bring over each time a few items of clothes or other things she wanted to use, to arrange things in the home, perform small tasks and simply savor the home. What I did was to make sure that she was covered whenever she made one of those trips. We got some idea of what she accomplished on those missions during her lifetime, but after her death we found out more. A striking example was when we were preparing for her wake, which was held at her home. We remembered that we would need white lace curtains, in keeping with the custom in those days of changing the curtains in a home to white lace curtains when a corpse was laid out, at least, in the parlor where the corpse was in repose and in areas adjacent to the parlor. Well, we found in her linen closet white lace curtains, washed, pressed, neatly folded and packed in a section of the closet. All we had to do was to hang them.

During her period with us, I left her free to do as much as she wanted to, mindful of the fact that she had always been very active. Henry watched with satisfaction and encouraged me not to stop her from doing things she wanted to do, lest she, as he put it, "die from inactivity." Yes, there was much to keep her occupied - to the extent that she was able. There were personal things to be done for herself and there was oversight of the children during working hours when they were out of school and I was at work at the University of Liberia. She took over automatically.

Naturally, there was much for us to share and I enjoyed her company as she did mine. I was still a comparatively young widow at the time and she showed a continuing concern for me. Sometimes, it seems she wondered if I would marry again. I guess she hoped so, but she did not live to see the day. It was almost three years after her death that on Jan. 1, 1973, I married George Flamma Sherman, then a Cabinet Minister in the Cabinet of President William R. Tolbert, Jr. He had previously given years of dedicated service in the diplomatic service of our country, in local government and in education.

Over time, the trips she made to her home decreased and tapered off. Although she never expressed it, we could feel the lessening of her desire to return there to live. Of course, she enjoyed spending more time with me, her grandsons, K.B. and Marbue, and her grandniece, Jebeh Freeman, daughter of Aunty Pai's son, Momo, who had become a part of my extended family following the death of Lducia in April, 1967. Moreover, her interaction and involvement with the children on a daily basis had its challenges. Besides, her health was beginning to fail and she realized it. As her strength lessened and her energy decreased, she seemed less and less inclined to contend with the steps of the long stairway leading from the entry of her three-story home to the second floor, the living quarters of the home. She found it much easier getting in and out of our much smaller ranch type house and moving about in it.

As she did so, her Christian faith continued to be her buttressing force. It provided her the strength she needed and was a major force in keeping her cheerful, even in the months ahead when her health worsened. Standing by were her own and the foster children, their spouses and children; her sister and other close relatives; and friends who visited more and kept her company as she moved around less and less. For some time, she also had as a companion the "Talking Book," audio tapes of the Holy Bible, sent to her by Antoinette (nickname Nettie) Tubman,[42] daughter of Mary Barclay Padmore and Stanley Padmore and wife of President William V.S. Tubman. The "Talking Book" was a source of hours of inspirational listening for her.

It was indeed a blessing that she suffered no ill effects to her eyesight from her diabetes. She remained the keen observer she always was up to her death. For example, I recall that when she returned home once after spending some time in the Cooper Clinic, she remarked that her room looked light. Well, I had had it painted while she was away and although it was in the same shade of pale pink, she noticed the fine difference the painting made.

A problem which persisted and increasingly bothered her as time went by was a bunion on one foot, which necessitated her wearing sandals and open shoes, even for dress occasions, rather than the closed and more stylish shoes she had been accustomed to wearing. She did not like this at all. Every now and then, she would talk about the bunion she had had removed in 1951 at the Deaconess Hospital in Boston when she was there to look into the management of her diabetes. Now, the other foot was giving her trouble and she began thinking of having the bunion removed. We tried to discourage her, pointing out that she was now advanced in years and had had the problem of diabetes for far more years than in 1951. But, we were not successful. She never completely put this thought out of her mind and simply waited for what to her seemed an opportune time.

As the months went by, we noticed that she began to experience problems which we saw as bigger. One of them related to her sense of time. For example, from the time we knew her and up to this point, she hardly ever slept during the day unless she was ill, which she seldom was. At this stage, she would occasionally fall asleep when it was daytime and when she awakened, she would sometimes think it was a new day. This posed some difficulties because she felt the regular routine of the day should start again and it was hard to convince her otherwise. A degree of bowel incontinence also began to rear its head and a change in the color of her stool made her doctor wonder if there was intestinal bleeding. He suggested exploratory surgery to determine whether there was cancer of the intestines. She would have no part of this and we went along with her in view of her age and particularly because of her diabetic condition. We wondered whether she would be able to heal from a major surgery such as this. In fact, our hope was that she would stay away from any surgery.

She was, however, insistent about removal of the bunion and her doctor felt this could be safely done and might be a step toward acceptance of the more major surgery. So, she went ahead with the surgery and it was declared successful. But, the larger problem was still there and so were its telltale effects. Before she could heal sufficiently to leave the Clinic, there was a breakdown in one part of the body and then another and her condition steadily deteriorated. It soon began to look like she would have to remain in the Clinic indefinitely. Treatment continued, but she did not return to normal. Nevertheless, we opted to take her back to the home environment she had become accustomed to. Although we tried, we could not find the professional nurses for the round the clock nursing care her doctor thought might be necessary. So, we settled for some professional nursing care, the rest to be done by ourselves and aides. We were blessed to secure the services of a professional nurse, Matilda Sisusa, for one shift each day, mainly overnight. The change of environment worked wonders for Ma's outlook and everything else; also Matilda related very well to her. Our overall arrangement worked fine. Gradually, there was an improvement in her condition, to her doctor's amazement and ours. However, from then on, she was practically confined to the home. There was also a marked decrease in her activity. Nevertheless, she was able to enjoy a number of months with us before she experienced problems that necessitated her return to the Clinic in March, 1970. That was her final trip to the Clinic.

During her confinement there, she was cheered by visits from us, Aunty Pai and other close relatives. (Aunty Mai had predeceased her.) Although quite sick, she was cheerful much of the time. Whenever she was asked how she felt, to our surprise, her response invariably was "all right." To the end, she stood strong, not given to complaining. She also continued to be discerning, shifting from one language to the other, depending on who she was talking to -- English as she spoke to us, the doctor, nurses and most people, Vai, as she conversed with her sister. But, "the end of us all," which she often spoke about, was drawing near for her.

Interestingly, her 12-year old granddaughter, Joy, would have a premonition. A couple of nights before she died, Joy had a dream which she related to her father the next morning. In the dream, she saw her grandfather come to their house, all dressed up. He asked that his grandchildren be brought and introduced to him. Remembering that he was dead, she stayed in the background, kept holding back and asking, "Isn't he dead?" As her father prodded her to come forward, she heard her grandfather tell him to leave her. After a while, she saw her grandfather escorting out of the house her grandmother, who was also all dressed up. The dream made her father feel that our mother's death was imminent, especially as the clothes, which from Joy's description her grandfather was wearing, were the same clothes he was laid out in at the time of his death 21 years earlier.

Well, it was the next day, Sunday, April 19, 1970, just after noon when she died at the Cooper Clinic where she had laid ill for about a month.

There were two days of wake keeping, April 21 and April 22, both days at her home. On the earlier date, President Tubman held an investiture in the parlor where her body lay and, for the Government of Liberia, conferred on her posthumously the decoration of Grand Cordon in the Most Venerable Order of the Pioneers (GCMVOP). Wanting to do even more, he had offered the Centennial Pavilion for her body to lie in state, but the family did not accept the offer, because we believed that she would have preferred to be laid out in her home and also we did not wish to have too much movement of her body. It was enough that President Tubman had honored her during her life, extending her courtesies she deserved as the widow of a Chief Justice. At official functions, for example, he always saw to it that she was seated at the head table where he sat.

The funeral service for her was held on Thursday, April 23, at Trinity Cathedral and interment followed at the Palm Grove Cemetery, Center Street, Monrovia. As the funeral procession wended its way from the Cathedral to the Cemetery, I could not help thinking of the words which she had used on a number of occasions when there was a death or funeral in the community of which she was aware -- "the end of us all." Death had indeed claimed her and we, her close ones, faced the reality of a physical separation from her. It was a sad time for us all, but we believed that God had given her eternal rest. And we knew that in our hearts and minds she would live on with love and warmth until the time came for each of us to die and join her.

CHAPTER 11

A Summing Up

Victoria Elizabeth Jellemoh was a remarkable person. With God at the center of her life, she stood for Christian principles and radiated a warm and vibrant personality. In simple ways, she wrote her name into the hearts of those whose lives she touched. A representative in her time of the best of the two worlds in Liberia - the indigenous and the Western oriented - she maintained strong ties in both of these worlds and contributed to bringing them together.

To a large extent, she was defined by her time. Thus, she saw herself primarily as a wife and a mother and endeavored to play those roles well. Testimony to her impact as a wife is reflected in the esteem in which her beloved Louis held her throughout their marriage and the fact that he felt he would be lost trying to live without her. He indicated this latter fact by expressing a preference to precede her in death. Her success as a mother was sung both by her own children and the children she fostered. I smile sometimes when I think that long after I left the hearth, I could, as the occasion warranted, literally hear some witty expression of hers and feel myself adhering to the principle it taught. I remember her with much love and affection. Indeed, I share my older brother Henry's belief that she was "a good, wise and understanding mother. . ."

Family had an important place in her life -- the larger family as well. Her dedication to it was strong. Like the true African, she experienced in her life and reflected that family provided love and warmth always and security from birth to death.

Early in her life, she reached out in service to her church, her community and later on, to her nation as well. These roles claimed a larger share of her attention as she reached her 60s and her responsibilities to her children diminished and to her husband were transformed with his death. Service was a way of acknowledging her blessings from God and expressing her concern for people. It was a way of releasing her creative talents. It brought her much joy and enhanced her sense of identity and purpose for living.

An outstanding Liberian historian, C. E. Zamba Liberty, marvels that she could be at the center of things in the nation almost all her life yet remain relatively unaffected. Her ability to maintain the common touch he saw as a major strength.

Of the generation of her grandson, Jim and a classmate of his also, he got to know her from his youth. It was as far back as that time that he began to observe the respect that she was accorded in various circles in Liberian society, a respect she would always enjoy. Indeed, she held her own among the high yet walked in friendship and love among the low.

Someone who knew her for a longer period of time was Corinna Hilton van Ee, daughter of a close friend of hers who herself grew to prominence in our country. She remembers her from the time she was a few years old until her death. She watched her as she grew up in Monrovia and became even closer to her in her adult years. Truly impressed by her, she remembers her with warmth and affection. "Glamour Girl" was the nickname she gave her when she was in her 60s and this she called her until her death. It was suggestive of how she carried herself - a role model in the community, proper in behavior and manners as well as in dress. When Corinna was providing me information on the Culture Club of Monrovia, she summed up her impressions of her simply, "and your mamma, lived her name" (Letter from Corinna dated Aug. 24, 1995). I couldn't help thinking of the fact that my mother felt strongly that a person's actions reflected what that person was and stood for. True to that, she did not think much of people who tried to show off. And, for her, the combination of birth in a "royal" clan and good breeding in a prominent family, complemented by marriage into a prominent family, meant that she would be humble, loving, warm and sensitive to people, naturally reflecting the best at all times. No doubt, her ingrained Christianity undergirded and reinforced these feelings.

From her vantage point, she transcended cleavages in the society along ethnic and class lines. It was not easy to do so at a time when integration in the society moved at a slow pace; also when those in high positions seemed unaware of or preferred to look askance rather than deal with the contradictions in the society. She and her husband can be credited not only for their stance in the society but also because they bequeathed the nation children (natural born and foster) with broad insights and sensitivities to the needs and challenges of a diverse society.

NOTES

[1] An expression coined by the Liberian novels and poet, Bai T. Moore. He designated Liberian life as a mixture of traditional values and the aspiration of a "sophisticated society." (Ofri-Scheps, "Bai T. Moore's Poetry and Liberian Identity"). p.20.

This society evolved through initiatives of the "New World" settlers, historically called Americo-Liberian, who pioneered the building of the Liberian State and   interaction with the indigenous ethnic groups which migrated to the area before them.

[2] Boakai H. Freeman, "The Vai and Their Kinsfolk," The Negro History Bulletin, Vol. 16, pp.60-62.

[3] Information from Jangaba Johnson, as reported by Ofri-Scheps, "On the Object of Ethnology: Apropos Vai Culture in Liberia," p.442.

[4] D. Elwood Dunn and Svend E. Holsoe, Historical Dictionary of Liberia, African Historical Dictionaries, No. 38 Metuchen, N. J. and London, The Scarecrow Press, 1985. p. 160.

[5] Op. Cit., Dunn and Holsoe, p. 162.

[6] The other four were the St. Paul, the Cestos, the Cavalla and the Sinoe. (See Schulze, pp. 183-184).

[7] Bronislaw Malinowski, Magic, Science and Religion and Others Essay, with Introduction by Robert Redfield. Doubleday Archor Books; Doubleday and Company, Garden City, New York, 1948, pp.17-18

[8] Maria Brierly, a descendant of Anglo-Scots, worked for 32 years in Africa-17 in Sierra Leone for the Church Missionary Society and 15 in Liberia for the Episcopal Church. Her work in Liberia was in the Cape Mount area among the Vais, Mendes and Golas.

She is remembered for being in the vanguard for getting the indigenous ethnic groups in the region where she worked to send their girls to the mission school (St. John's) and for promoting integration at the school between Americo-Lberian and indigenous girls. Mother Brierly, as she came to be called, was also known for her work among the poor and helpless. (See Beysolow, T. E., "Christian Missions and Their Propagators)."

[9] See "The Orphan Asylum and Girls School, Cape Palmas, Liberia, West Africa," Archives of the Episcopal Church in the United States of America, p.1.

[10] From the Course of Study of the Female Orphan Asylum, Cape Palmas, 1855, in "A Report of the Origin, Progress and Present Position of the Female Orphan Asylum At Cape Palmas, Philadelphia, Printed by King and Baird, 9 Sansom Street, 1856, Archives of the Episcopal Church in the USA, p.5.

[11] A Circular From The Board of Managers of the Cape Palmas Female Orphan Asylum To Their Friends and Patrons, Philadelphia: King and Baird, Printers, No 9 Sansom Street, 1856, p. 27, Archives of the Episcopal Church in the USA.

[12] *Ibid.*

[13] Spirit of Missions, vol. 61. 1896, p. 27, Archives of the Episcopal Church in the USA.

[14] *Ibid.*

[15] Elwood D. Dunn, A History of the Episcopal Church in Liberia, Metuchen, N.J. and London, The American Theological Library Association and the Scarecrow Press, 1992, p.92.

[16] That child, Ernest Marbue, was named Ernest after Louis' uncile, Ernest James Barclay and Marbue after her uncle, Chief Varney Marbue.

[17] At the time, the County Attorney for Montserrado County sometimes assisted the County Attorney in the other Counties in the prosecution of criminal cases (Information furnished by my brother, Rudolph, who, following in our father's footsteps, became a lawyer.)

[18] One sibling, Samuel Gerald, died in Barbados at age four, about 10 years before the family left for Liberia. See A nephew (Grimes, Louis Arthur), "A Brief Sketch of the Life of Malvina Barclay," p.5.

[19] The Barbadians who comprised this immigration were described as "the most intelligent and best-educated company of emigrants that ever came to Liberia and equally industrious." Cited from The African Repository, XLIX, September, 1873, p. 284, in Brown, "Education and National Development in Liberia," p. 157.

[20] Another member of Louis' graduating class of six, the 1903 Class of Liberia College, who heeded Blyden and married across ethic lines, was Abayomi Karnga. Isabella Klade Hodge who he selected as a bride and married in 1914 was Grebo. Karnga was a descendant of recaptures Africans returned to Liberia from the high seas.

[21] Edwin Barclay was the son of Louis' uncle, Ernest James Barclay, after whom his fourth son was given the name Ernest. See note 8, Chapter 2, p. 94.

[22] Ofri-Scheps, "On the Object of Ethnology: Apropos Vai Culture in Liberia," p. 3.

[23] Elizabeth Barclay and Mary Barclay were the children of Arthur Barclay and his first wife, Mary Marshall Barclay - whole sisters of Anthony Barclay.

[24] Karmo versus Morris, Liberian Law Reports, 2, pp. 317-334.

[25] Liberia was then divided into four coastal Counties (Montserrado, Grand Bassa, Sinoe and Maryland) and the area beyond the 40-mile limit of each County, referred to then as the hinterland, into three Provinces (Eastern, Central and Western). Cape Mount was then a part of Montserrado County.

[26] It is testimony to the independence and strength of the judiciary at the time that this decision was made against the Government. All of the justices on the Bench at the time were of settler descent. (For this information and insights provided on the Karmo versus Morris case, I am indebted to my brother, Rudolph).

[27] Measie is a Gola title of respect used by young girls to address their female elders.

[28] Family in Liberia is extended. Its membership varies, but it could include, in addition to parents and their natural born children was hardly thought of. Children, most of whom were of indigenous background, were entrusted to relatives, friends, prominent people and other people regarded as successful in the Liberian "sophisticated society," to be reared in their homes, but not given up to them in the Western sense of adoption.

[29] See Appendix V, page 105, for information on the children in the extended family and the natural born children of the couple. Unfortunately, I have not mentioned in the story five of the children in the extended family. This is due to my inability to place them in a precise time frame in the story. The five omitted are: Helen, Lapola, Dennch, Jimmy and Sumo Grimes.

[30] St. John then carried only elementary grades and stopped at grade eight. High school grades were added in 1934 and the school was called Episcopal High School.

[31] For the names of the members of the Club, see Appendix II, page 101.

[32] This building served as the Executive Mansion from 1848 to 1916, (Richardson, and page 121).

[33] The College of West Africa closed out its collegiate division about 1908. During the 1930s and 1949s, its program of studies covered grades four to 12.

[34] From about 4,000 thousand when Victoria came as a young wife, it was about 12,000. (For the population figures of Monrovia, see Schulze, page 85).

[35] Jackson Doe had the distinction of being the first person hailing from an indigenous ethnic group to be elected President of the nation. This was during the 1985 elections when exit polls showed that he won the election, his party, the Liberian Action Party (LAP). However, due to election fraud, he was never so declared and consequently, never assumed the position.

[36] For a compilation of these and other words of wisdom of my mother, as remembered by me-Vic's Guiding Words-see Appendix 4, pages 103-104.

[37] Mabel Keaton Staupers was of West Indian descent. She was born in Barbados, West Indies, Feb. 27, 1890, and immigrated to the United States of America, with her parents, in April, 1903. She worked assiduously for the integration of African American nurses into the mainstream of American nursing, leading the fight through the National Association of Colored Graduate Nurses (NACGN), of which she was Executive Secretary, 1934 to 1949. (See Darlene Clark Hines, "Mabel Keaton Staupers, 1890-1989," pages 1074-1077).

During Mabel Staupers' tenure as Executive Secretary, Marion Seymour was associated with the organization in the struggle to open opportunities for African American nurses to take graduate level courses in the Washington, D. C. areas.

[38] First cousins of Louis who grew up in Bassa County were: Emma Alberta Morgan (later Mrs. Joshua Davis: and Edwin Alford Morgan, children of his Aunt, Laura Ann Barclay Morgan; and Georgia Barclay, daughter of his Uncle, Anthony Barclay.

[39] Kedrick's Office was then based in New York City, although he was still serving as Financial Attaché of the Liberian Embassy. His responsibilities, in addition to the Embassy, included the Liberian Consulate General and the Liberian Permanent Mission to the United Nations which were based in New York City, and students in the United States who were receiving scholarship and financial aid from the Liberian Government.

[40] Arriving after her death were the adopted daughter of Henry and his second wife, Rosina - Merlene Grimes - and the adopted daughters of Rudolph and Doris - Dolly Grimes Johnson and Doris Grimes.

[41] Henry married Rosina Robinson, daughter of Mai Bright Robinson and Joshua Robinson February 5, 1966, his first marriage having ended in divorce in early 1964.

[42] My mother always had a warm spot in her heart for Nettie. One of the three babies born in the Barclay family between January, 1914, and March, 1914 (Irene Wiles in January, she in February and my mother's second child, Henry, in March), she was special to my mother from her birth up to my mother's death. She reciprocated these warm feelings.

BIBLIOGRAPHY

A Circular From The Board of Managers of the Cape Palmas Female Orphan Asylum To Their Friends and Patrons, Philadelphia: Printed By King & Baird, 9 Sansom Street, Archives of the Episcopal Church in the USA, 1856.

A Report of the Origin, Progress and Present Position of the Female Orphan Asylum, At Cape Palmas, Philadelphia, Printed by King & Baird, 9 Sansom Street, Archives of the Episcopal Church in the USA, 1856.

Beysolow, T. E., "Christian Missions and Their Propagators," *Liberian Churchman*, vol. II, June and August, 1924, nos. 5 and 6, pages 4-7, in Collection of the Honorable Louis Arthur Grimes, 1883-1948, available on microfilm from African Imprint Library Service, West Falmouth, MA. 6 reels.

Brown, Mary Antoinette Grimes, "Education and National Development in Liberia," unpublished Ph.D. thesis, Cornell University, 1967.

Collection of the Honorable Louis Arthur Grimes, 1883-1948, available on microfilm from the African Imprint Library Service, West Falmouth, MA, 6 reels.

Dunn, D. Elwood, *A History of the Episcopal Church in Liberia*, Metuchen, N.J. and London, The American Theological Library Association and The Scarecrow Press, 1992.

Dunn, D. Elwood and Svend E. Holsoe, *Historical Dictionary of Liberia*, African Historical Dictionaries, No. 38, Metuchen, N.J. & London, The Scarecrow Press, 1985.

Freeman, H. Boakai, "The Vai and Their Kinsfolk," *The Negro History Bulletin*, vol. 16, pages 51-63.

A nephew (Grimes, Louis A.), "A Brief Sketch of the Life of Malvina Barclay," unpublished manuscript, n.p., n.d.

Heard, William H., *The Bright Side of African Life*, New York, Negro Universities Press, A Division of Greenwood Publishing Corporation, 1969 (originally published in 1898 by the A.M.E. Publishing House, Philadelphia).

Hine, Darlene Clark, "Mabel Keaton Staupers (1890-1989)" *Notable Black American Women*, ed. Jessie Carney Smith, Detroit, London: Gale Research Inc., 1992.

Liberia Bulletin, No. 3, November, 1893.

Liberian Law Reports, Volume 2, Ithaca, New York, Cornell University Press, 1972.

Malinowski, Bronislaw, *Magic, Science and Religion and Other Essays*, with an Introduction by Robert Redfield, Doubleday Anchor Books, Doubleday and Company, Garden City, New York, 1948.

Ofri-Scheps, Dorith, "Bai T. Moore's Poetry and Liberian Identity," *Liberian Studies Journal*, vol. xv, no. 2, 1990.

Ofri-Scheps, Dorith, "On the Object of Ethnology: Apropos Vai Culture in Liberia," Ph. D. thesis, University of Berne, 1991.

Padmore, George Arthur, *The Memoirs of a Liberian Ambassador: George Arthur Padmore*, Lewiston, NY, The Edwin Mellon Press, 1996.

Richardson, Nathaniel R., *Liberia's Past and Present*, London, The Diplomatic Press and Publishing Company, 1959.

Schulze, Willi, *A New Geography of Liberia*, London, Longman Group Limited, 1973.

Spirit of Missions, vols. 61 and 65, 1896 and 1900, Archives of the Episcopal Church of the USA.

The Liberia Official Gazette, vol. xxx, No. 12, Wednesday, Dec. 15, 1948.

The Liberia Official Gazette, vol. xlix, No. 4, Thursday, April 23, 1970.

The University of Liberia Register of Graduates, Centennial Issue, Monrovia, 1962.

APPENDIX I

In the Name ✠ of the Father, and of the Son, and of the Holy Ghost, Amen.

This is to Certify, that

on the _tenth_ day of _December_ in the Year of **Our Lord**, One Thousand, Nine Hundred and _eleven_ at _Mechlin House_ in the _city_ of _Edina, Grand Bassa County,_ I joined together in

HOLY MATRIMONY

Louis Arthur Grimes and

Mr. Victoria E. Cheeseman,

according to the Form of Solemnization of Matrimony as contained in the Book of Common Prayer, and in Conformity with the Laws of the _Republic_ of _Liberia_ ~~United States of America~~

In Witness Whereof, I have hereunto affixed my name this _eleventh_ day of _December_ One Thousand, Nine Hundred and _eleven_

Witnesses:

T. O. Jucannus K. Russell
Rector of St. John's.

Anthony Barclay

Eliza Ray Jackson

APPENDIX II

MEMBERS OF THE CULTURE CLUB OF MONROVIA
(Organized in Monrovia around 1918[1])

Euphemia Barclay

Sarah Raynes Barclay

Clara A. Cassell

Harriet George

Victoria E. Grimes

M. Eva McGill Hilton

Isabella K. Karnga

Matilda M. Parker

F. Mai Wiles

---

1. Information furnished by Corinna Hilton van Ee.

APPENDIX III

TRIBUTE TO MY MOTHER
VICTORIA ELIZABETH GRIMES

I have an inspiring and affectionate memory of Victoria Elizabeth Grimes, a good, wise and understanding Mother to her own five and to the many whom she reared.

Born under unpretentious circumstances, she was lucky to have been chosen and reared under more preferred environment. And, always remembering her own good fortune, she tried to help and uplift as many of similar origins, as she could. Not fortunate to have access to the higher disciplines, she, nevertheless, had an awareness of the potential that could be unleashed by a result of high intellectual pursuits. Thus, at home, she was the encouragement and the driving force in the education of her own and of her extended family. She accepted no excuse for poor grades.

She was a devout Christian and conducted daily family prayers. She believed no matter how rough the going, right must triumph over wrong. She prayed for strength to do the hard right as against the easy wrong; for courage to hold to your honest convictions as against the sacrifices of principles for expediency or gain; for contentment with your honest lot as against the intrigues of the lure of wealth.

She believed her purpose was to serve her family, her Church, her Community and social societies she was connected with. To these, she endeavored to give her best efforts during her lifetime.

May she enjoy her rest in heavenly repose.

Written by
Henry W. Grimes on
Mother's Day,
May 14, 1978.

APPENDIX IV

VIC'S GUIDING WORDS

1. "Mr. Talk" is all right, but "Dr. do" is the man.
2. Hold God to His promises.
3. God fits the back for the burden.
4. Don't take the last pea out of the pod.
5. Go to the seashore and fill both of your hands with sand. Close one tightly and leave the other open. When you open the closed hand, you will find that it has less sand than the hand which remained open.
6. If you only have salt and cassava, eat that and be thankful to god. Make no complaint.
7. Don't carry the "lazy man's load."
8. Avoid "giving other people's children hands and feet and taking them from your own children."
9. You are "looking for work and praying to God not to find it."
10. Don't put on "jackass" airs like the peacock.
11. "Braggart" was a good dog, but "Hold Fast" was the better dog.
12. When you do your best, no more is required.
13. All money is not good money.
14. Liquor in, wits out.
15. See and don't see.
16. There are two kinds of kinjahs - those you can rest and those you can not rest.
17. The dead have no power.
18. Don't be surprise at what happens; be surprised at what doesn't happen
19. All cry do for burial.
20. Be careful how you lend money. You may be paying to break a friendship.
21. If you buy me for a fool, you won't sell me for one.

--From the memory of Mary Antoinette Hope

APPENDIX V

CHILDREN OF LOUIS ARTHUR GRIMES AND
VICTORIA ELIZABETH JELLEMOH GRIMES[1]
(Ethnic backgrounds indicated)

Natural Born		Children comprising the extended family	
Louis Arthur Grimes, Jr.	mixed[2]	Elsie Frank	Kru
Henry Waldron Grimes	mixed	Peter Hall	Bassa
Joseph Rudolph Grimes	mixed	William Grimes	Bassa
Mary Antoinette Hope Grimes	mixed	Charlotte Madea Grimes	Bassa
Ernest Marbue Grimes	mixed	Emmett Harmon	Settler
		Edna Zoe Mayers	Gola
		Lasanah Grimes	Kpelle
		Christine Morgan	Settler
		Garbeah Grimes	Bassa
		Gladys Smith	mixed[3]
		Albert Kini Freeman	Vai
		George Molondoi Freeman	Vai
		James Rudolph Grimes[4]	mixed
		Momo Freeman	Vai
		Mary Zina Freeman	Vai
		Jackson Fiah Doe	Gio
		Helen	?
		Lapolah	?
		Sumo Grimes	?
		Denneh	Kpelle
		Jimmy	Kpelle

1. Natural born children are listed in the order of their birth; children in the extended family in the approximate order in which they became a part of the home.

2. Settler and indigenous background. In the case of each of the five natural born children, the ethnic background is settler and Vai.

3. Settler and indigenous background. In this case, the ethnic background is settler and Bassa.

4. The first grandchild of the couple; he was reared by them from one year old. His background is settler/Vai and settler/Bassa.

President J.J. Cheeseman

Mrs. J.J. Cheeseman

The Foster Parents of Victoria Elizabeth Jellemoh

Louis Arthur Grimes
Husband of
Victoria Elizabeth Jellemoh

Henry Waldron

Mary Antoinette Hope

Joseph Rudolph

*The three children of Louis Arthur Grimes
and Victoria Elizabeth Jellemoh Grimes
who survived to maturity*

*Albert Kini Freeman
Son of Victoria's sister
Hawa Pai*

Charlotte Madea Grimes

Edna Zoe Freeman

Jackson Fiah Poe

*Four of the children in the extended family
in their adult years*

Victoria Elizabeth Jellemoh with her daugther, Mary Antoinette and her son-in-law, Kedrick Brown in Washington, D.C., 1951

Jim Grimes

Joy Grimes

Pearl Grimes

Lducia Brown   *Marbue Brown*   *Kedrick W. Brown Jr. (K.B.)*

The six grandchildren Victoria Elizabeth Jellemoh was blessed to see

*Grimes Home,
Broad Street, Monrovia, Liberia
November, 1997- After repairs
following the damages sustained
during the civil war of 1989-1996
Initially occupied December 1912,
Remodeled during the 1950s and
1960s*

*Orphan Asylum and Girls School
Cape Palmas, c 1887
(Photo courtesy of the archives
of the Episcopal Church)*

*Cape Palmas Asylum and Lighthouse
Cape Palmas, Africa
(Photo courtesy of the archives
of the Episcopal Church)*

*Brierley Memorial Hall,
Cape Palmas
(Photo courtesy of the archives
of the Episcopal Church)*

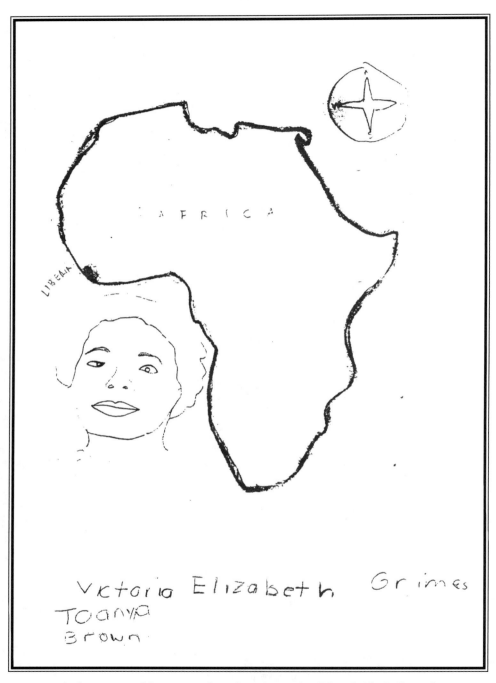

*A drawing of her grandmother Victoria Elizabeth Jellemoh
beside the map of Africa
By Taanya Mokandai Brown, age 7*